FORECASTING MODELS FOR NATIONAL ECONOMIC PLANNING

A. R. G. HEESTERMAN

FORECASTING MODELS
FOR NATIONAL ECONOMIC
PLANNING

GORDON AND BREACH / SCIENCE PUBLISHERS

NEW YORK

PUBLISHED IN THE NETHERLANDS BY
D. REIDEL PUBLISHING COMPANY
PUBLISHED IN THE UNITED STATES BY
GORDON AND BREACH
SCIENCE PUBLISHERS, INC.
150 Fifth Avenue, New York, N.Y. 10011

Printed in The Netherlands by D. Reidel, Dordrecht

ACKNOWLEDGEMENTS

I started the writing of this book as mimeographed lecture notes. As a result, my first acknowledgement should go to my students, both the (then) undergraduates in my Econometrics class, and the postgraduates in National Economic Planning. They were the people, who, more than anybody else, influenced the content, first by discussion of the material during lectures before the notes were even fully written, and later by requests for clarification on specific topics, and at a still later stage, by noticing any errors in the text and formulae, such as wrong indices, erroneous numbering, etc.

I should then mention the encouragement of my colleagues, especially of my friend and temporary Acting Head of the Department, Dr. H. Neudecker. The next acknowledgement goes to Mrs. L. Fowles and Mrs. B. Barlow for reading my handwriting and typing the manuscript.

Furthermore, I am indebted to Mr. R. W. Bayliss, my student at the time, who will presumably be M.Soc.Sc. (National Economic Planning), when this book comes out, and to Mr. A. Irving, a co-member of the staff at this University, for correcting the English, this not being my native language.

A. R. G. HEESTERMAN

14.8.69, University of Birmingham, England

TABLE OF CONTENTS

TABLE OF CONTENTS

TABLE OF CONTENTS

PREFACE AND INTRODUCTION

This book is about the specification of linear econometric models, and for this reason some important related fields have been deliberately omitted. I did not want to discuss the problems of parameter-estimation, at least not in any detail, as there are other books on these problems written by specialized statisticians. This book is about the models themselves and macro-economic models in particular. A second related subject is the policy decision that can be made with the help of a model. While I did write a chapter on policy decisions, I limited myself to some extent because of my views on planning as such. The logical approach to this problem is in terms of mathematical programming, but our models and our ideas about the policies we want are too crude for its effective utilisation. A realistic formulation of the problem should involve non-linearities in an essential way, the models I consider (and most existing models) are linear. At the present state of econometrics, I do not really believe in such a thing as the 'optimal' plan. The possible result of bad planning or no planning at all, for instance massive unemployment, sudden financial crises, unused capital equipment, or the production of unsalable goods is agreed to be undesirable. Programming methods may of course be needed, if only for having a systematic algorithm to find a solution that avoids this kind of 'obvious' non-optimality. However, the main emphasis is on forecasting models. To frame policy, bearing in mind such knowledge about the future and the likely impact of our own actions on future events to the best of our ability, is an attempt to behave rationally.

I have tried to write a book which gives a reasonable coverage of existing models, or rather the existing types of models and sub-models. The description of actual models was limited by the following considerations: First of all, unavoidably, by the limits of my knowledge, this may have given rise to some bias in the presentation.

It was not, however, my purpose to give a representative survey of all published models and types of model, where I have discussed actual

1

published models and not those created by me for the purpose of illustration, they are still basically meant as 'examples'. It was not my intention to write a book about 'models' in their abstract form, but a book which might be of some help in constructing models, particularly to an individual who wants to construct a model for the first time. This requires a fairly detailed discussion of at least some of the conceivable types of relations which can be found in certain categories of models. At the same time, I have tried to provide at least a basic coverage of models 'in general', by ordering them according to specific criteria. In a sense, this was of course a limitation on the subject matter; models which did not easily fit into this classification, were automatically unsuitable for discussion as an example to illustrate the principles covered. The classification was done by means of the following criteria: the first was 'short-term' versus 'long-term' and since I did not discuss either seasonal fluctuation or seasonal adjustment, quarterly models fell outside the book. I have had very little experience with them and so 'short-term' in this work means on an annual basis. The second criterion was macro model vs. sectorized model. For both the criteria I have described what are in my opinion the essential points in the specification of the model which emerge in belonging to either one or the other grouping.

The short vs. long criterion is essentially the treatment of the demand for production factors, and the explicit description of dynamic adjustment mechanisms (accelerator and lagged response reactions) or their replacement by equilibrium conditions. In the case of the macro vs. sectorized criterion, the distinction here lies in the accounting framework on which the model is based. For the macro model these are (additative) macro-economic accounting balances and for the sectorized model this is the input-output table. As far as the sectorized model has any definite shape, it also incorporates some of the restrictive assumptions of the Leontief input-output model. A specific sectorized model is best described by reference to the input-output model. The points can be listed where it does not follow the restrictive assumptions of the traditional Leontief model and the additional relations, which are introduced in order to 'close' the model, can be enumerated.

Logically, the above classification admits to four types of models as follows: Macro-economic short term models, macro-economic long term models, sectorized short term models and sectorized long term models.

2

The majority of the existing models belong to only two of these four types, the macro-economic short term model and the sectorized long term model. I have tried to give a description of the 'typical' model belonging to either of these groups by discussing the major problems associated with each. There are of course models which do not answer any of the descriptions given by me, but as far as this concerns short term forecasting models, I can only say 'so much the worse for such a model'. I believe the type of short term model I describe to be well established. In addition its main elements; expenditure multipliers, accelerator mechanisms and lagged response reactions, have a more or less recognized place in current business cycle theory outside econometric model building.

Considerable effort would be saved by anyone wanting to construct a short term forecasting model if he more or less adheres to the description in Chapter II. Furthermore, I want to defend the desirability of some degree of normalization of models, even where we do not find that existing models are satisfactory. When I see a model for the first time, I wish to 'understand' what the model says, in terms of a verbal description of the assumptions of economic theory, this is not always an easy task with a large model. Now if we could agree to describe our models in relation to their differences and agreements with certain more or less standardized types, this would save considerable effort in the reading and writing of papers. Unfortunately, there is not as yet a generally accepted type of sectorized model, but I have tried to describe some possible variations of the traditional Leontief input-output model. The introductory chapters of the book do not assume previous knowledge of related fields such as statistics, mathematics, etcetera. Later chapters gradually assume more knowledge of related fields. In this respect the book was specifically written for students who are at the same time studying other related subjects.

CHAPTER I

THE BASIC CONCEPTS OF LINEAR MODELS

1.1. ECONOMIC EQUATION SYSTEMS

What is a model? Generally a model is a representation of something else, which is a real phenomenon. The purpose of such a representation is to facilitate the study and understanding of the real phenomenon. The model may be easier to see, nearer by, or less dependent on time, relative to the real phenomenon. A shipbuilder may make a small-scale model of a ship he intends to build. In this case the real phenomenon does not as yet exist but many properties of the ship can be studied on the scale-model. In econometrics, the concept of a model has a more precise meaning. The model is a system of equations, representing a particular aspect of reality, or supposed reality. The representation of a not as yet existing structure is one of the useful applications of models, this is true both for the shipbuilder and for the econometrician. Computer simulation of the results of proposed changes in fiscal legislation or monetary policy may be helpful in deciding whether or not to introduce such changes. The concept of a model as a system of equations, representing a simulated reality, is valid for such varied applications as engineering, weather forecasting and outerspace navigation.

The word 'econometric' restricts the application to economic phenomena. An econometric model is a system of equations, representing a certain economic phenomenon, or complex of economic phenomena.

1.2. SOME CONVENTIONS OF NOTATION

The notation used for linear models is considerably simplified by the adoption of matrix notation[1], in addition a concise and systematic notation considerably facilitates the analysis of linear systems. For this reason, matrix notation will be used throughout this book wherever possible. However, examples of certain types of models will be written in extenso. Where matrix notation is used, the following conventions will be adhered to: Matrices will be indicated with capital letters (upper case), e.g. A, C, X. The corresponding lower-case letter, with two indices, will then indicate an element of the matrix, the first index being the row-index, the second one the column index, i.e. a_{ij} for an element of A. In matrix-formulae, lower-case letters without indices will always be themselves indices, such as order-parameters, row-indices, etc. Single constants of a non-integer type will be indicated with Greek letters. Vectors will be indicated with lower-case letters, in heavy print e.g. $\mathbf{a}'$, or $\mathbf{b}'$. Vectors will be indicated as columns and row vectors will always have a prime ($\mathbf{a}$ for a column, $\mathbf{a}'$ for a row). Columns of a matrix will be indicated with the corresponding lower-case letter in heavy print, with a single index. The same symbol with a prime will be a row of the matrix and transposed columns must therefore be indicated within brackets. Hence, $\mathbf{a}_j$ is the jth column of A, $\mathbf{a}'_j$ is the jth row of A, and $(\mathbf{a}_j)'$ is the jth column of A, transposed into a row-vector. Similarly $(\mathbf{a}'_i)'$ will be the ith row of A, transposed into a column. Order-parameters need only be stated explicitly where they are not self-evident. Hence, if we write the expression $A\mathbf{x}$, and state that A is of order m by n, then the further information that $\mathbf{x}$ is a vector of order n by 1 need not be stated explicitly. Order parameters may be lower-case letters, numbers or lower-case letters with a single index. It is possible to suppress order-parameters altogether. The mere writing of the expression

$$A\mathbf{x} = \mathbf{b}$$

will inform us of the fact that A is a matrix, and $\mathbf{x}$ and $\mathbf{b}$ column vectors; and also that the order of $\mathbf{x}$ is equal to the number of columns of A, and the order of $\mathbf{b}$ equal to the number of rows in A. When partitioning matrices we will adhere to the following conventions: A block-column of a matrix will be indicated by the corresponding upper-case letter, the same as for the matrix, with a single index. A block-row will be indicated in the same way, but with a prime. Here we follow the same system as for individual rows and columns; A_j will be the jth block-column of A; $(A_j)'$ the transpose of the jth block-column and $(A'_i)'$ the transpose of the ith block-row. If the order-parameters of the parent-matrix are known, the order of a block-column is determined by stating its number of columns. If it was already stated that B is of order p by q and we now introduce the block-column B_2, which is of order p by q_2, we need only state that B_2 has

q_2 columns. A lower-case letter with a single index will always be an order-parameter of a block, block-row or block-column, the same letter without index being the corresponding parameter of the parent-matrix. Partitioning of a matrix will automatically define the partitioning of any vectors, which may be used in one expression with the matrix. Hence, if we already used the expression $A\mathbf{x}$ where A is of order m by n and now partition A into two block-columns, A_1 of n_1 columns and A_2 of n_2 columns, we have also stated that $\mathbf{x}$ is of order n and is partitioned into two subvectors, of orders n_1 and n_2.

The above conventions will all be subject to ad-hoc variation. Different notations will be introduced for specific formulae, or in certain sections, if useful. Such non-conventional notation will be defined at the appropriate place in the text where it is introduced. One general exception which should be mentioned here, is that when individual economic relationships are discussed in terms of their economic significance the conventions for matrix notation will not be applicable. We will then use any letters or combinations of letters, whether or not such symbols have a specific use in matrix notation. Generally, economic variables will be indicated by means of a few letters, forming an abbreviation of the English word for the corresponding variable written in extenso. Where capital letters are used, they will refer to money flows[2], the corresponding lower-case letters indicating value in constant prices.

A further point concerns the numbering of the formulae. In order to facilitate references to formulae, each formula will be indicated by three numbers; the first number indicating the chapter to which it belongs, the second the section, and the third number giving the ordering within the section. Equations belonging to examples have a separate numbering system, indicated by the additional insertion of the letters ex for example in the formula-identifier. Then (5.3.4) is the fourth formula in the main text of Section 5.3; there may also be an Equation (5.3.ex.4) in the same section, which is the fourth equation of the example in Section 5.3.

1.3. THE BASIC BLOCK-EQUATION

Economic variables can be grouped into two vectors. One vector of variables is explained by means of the model and these are the 'endogenous' or 'jointly dependent' variables. The other group of variables are

6

not explained by the model, but are needed for a quantitative explanation of the dependent variables. They are not in themselves considered to be dependent on the jointly dependent variables. These variables are named 'predetermined' or 'exogenous' variables.

The most general specification of the linear model will be

$$A\mathbf{y} = B\mathbf{x}. \qquad (1.3.1.)$$

Here $\mathbf{y}$ is the vector of jointly dependent variables, $\mathbf{x}$ the vector of exogenous variables, A and B will be matrices of coefficients. To have a meaningful model at all, we require A to be square and non-singular. The relation (1.3.1) is in fact a simplification of

$$A\mathbf{y}_t = B\mathbf{x}_t + \mathbf{u}_t, \qquad (1.3.2.)$$

where $\mathbf{u}$ is a vector of random error terms from the estimation of the relationships. Problems of estimating models are not as such the subject-matter of this book. We will treat our coefficients as known, if necessary after application of suitable statistical techniques. When the model is applied to the future, the random error is replaced by its expectation which is zero, this to all practical purposes reduces (1.3.2) back into (1.3.1).

Example
Consider the following business-cycle model: In substance, this model is chiefly attributable to Harrod and Hicks (see Hicks [28].).

This model is written out below, with some alterations which are as follows: (a) The production balance has been completed to include government expenditure; (b) an exogenous term, representing autonomous investment has been added to the investment relation; and (c) a tax-variable has been introduced.

The notation has been adjusted to the conventions described above. The Hicks-Harrod model refers to a closed economy so there is no foreign trade. In this simplified model, there is no stock formation, except possibly as part of investment. As a result, there are only 3 final demand categories, consumption, investment and government expenditure on goods and services. In the original Hicks-Harrod model, there is no taxation but this has been changed. The adjusted model contains separate variables for production and spendable income. To illustrate the model, numerical values for the coefficients have been filled in. These numbers have been chosen in a plausible order of magnitude, but have no statistical basis. The model is now as follows:

List of variables[3]

A. *Jointly Dependent Variables*

p_t,   production in the current period

si_t,   spendable income of the citizens, in the current period

c_t,   private consumption, in the current period

i_t,   investment, in the current period

B. *Exogenous Variables*

g_t,   government's expenditure on goods and services, in the current period

tfm_t, tax free minimum; the level of productive income at which net tax is zero; in the current period

iau_t, autonomous investment, in the current period

p_{t-1}, production in the previous period

p_{t-2}, production, two periods back.

The Equations

production balance:

$$p_t = c_t + i_t + g_t \qquad\qquad (1.3.\text{ex.}1)$$

fiscal relation:

$$si_t = 0.75\,(p_t - tfm_t) + tfm_t \qquad\qquad (1.3.\text{ex.}2)$$

consumption function:

$$c_t = 0.80 si_t \qquad\qquad (1.3.\text{ex.}3)$$

investment function:

$$i_t = 2\,(p_{t-1} - p_{t-2}) + iau_t. \qquad\qquad (1.3.\text{ex.}4)$$

To conform to (1.3.1) we group all terms referring to the jointly dependent variables onto the left-hand side; leaving only terms referring to exogenous variables on the right-hand side. We therefore obtain the following equations:

$$p_t - c_t - i_t = g_t$$
$$si_t - 0.75p_t = 0.25tfm_t$$
$$c_t - 0.80si_t = 0$$
$$i_t = 2\left(p_{t-1} - p_{t-2}\right) + iau_t$$

The model may now be written as follows:

TABLE I

	p_t	si_t	c_t	i_t	$=$	g_t	tfm_t	iau_t	p_{t-1}	p_{t-2}
(1)	1.00	–	– 1.00	– 1.00		1.00	–	–	–	–
(2)	– 0.75	1.00	–	–		–	0.25	–	–	–
(3)	–	– 0.80	1.00	–		–	–	–	–	–
(4)	–	–	–	1.00		–	–	1.00	2.00	– 2.00

From Table I of the coefficients, we now readily identify the matrices A and B and the vectors $\mathbf{y}$ and $\mathbf{x}$ out of (1.3.1)

$$A = \begin{bmatrix} 1.00 & - & -1.00 & -1.00 \\ -0.75 & 1.00 & & - \\ - & -0.80 & 1.00 & - \\ - & - & - & 1.00 \end{bmatrix}$$

$$\mathbf{y} = \begin{bmatrix} p_t \\ si_t \\ c_t \\ i_t \end{bmatrix}$$

$$B = \begin{bmatrix} 1.00 & - & - & - & - \\ - & 0.25 & - & - & - \\ - & - & - & - & - \\ - & - & 1.00 & 2.00 & -2.00 \end{bmatrix}$$

and

$$\mathbf{x} = \begin{bmatrix} g_t \\ tfm_t \\ iau_t \\ p_{t-1} \\ p_{t-2} \end{bmatrix}$$

9

Or, writing (1.3.1) out explicitly

$$
\begin{bmatrix}
1.00 & - & -1.00 & -1.00 \\
-0.75 & 1.00 & - & - \\
- & -0.80 & 1.00 & - \\
- & - & - & 1.00
\end{bmatrix}
\begin{bmatrix}
p_t \\ si_t \\ c_t \\ i_t
\end{bmatrix}
=
$$

$$
\begin{bmatrix}
1.00 & - & - & - & - \\
- & 0.25 & - & - & - \\
- & - & - & - & - \\
- & - & 1.00 & 2.00 & -2.00
\end{bmatrix}
\begin{bmatrix}
g_t \\ tfm_t \\ iau_t \\ p_{t-1} \\ p_{t-2}
\end{bmatrix}
$$

The above model will be used as an illustrative example, throughout the rest of this chapter.

1.4. SOME TYPES OF RELATIONS

Economic relations can be classified into a number of different types[4], notably:

Definition identities. These relations are known to be as they are, by logic. An example is (1.3.ex.1) in the previous section.

$$p_t = c_t + i_t + g_t$$

is as it is, because within the accounting framework underlying the model, this is so by definition. The relation

$$p_t = 0.98c_t + 1.01i_t + 1.02g_t$$

written instead of (1.3.ex.1) would just be untrue.

Institutional relationships. These relations are as they are, because that is how society is organized. If desirable, they could be changed, by altering the relevant institutional arrangements. An example is the fiscal relation (1.3.ex.2) in the previous section.

The relation

$$si_t = 0.75 \, (p_t - tfm_t) + tfm_t$$

is as it is, because fiscal regulations specify a net taxation of 25% of all gross income, in excess of the tax-free minimum. This type of relation, once written down as a linear function of aggregate accounting variables, is in fact a considerable simplification of the true set of regulations. Fiscal regulations are not as simple as assumed by (1.3.ex.2). Tax liability of economic subjects does not just depend on income. Factors of personal status, such as age, married or single, in good health or disabled, are taken into account as well. Even if the individual tax liability should be as simple as assumed by (1.3.ex.2) there would be consistency differences between tax due on transaction basis, as arising from the earned income and the actual tax paid in the same period. All these factors will give rise to a residual error in (1.3.ex.2), even if the relevant regulations are precisely known.

Reaction equations. This is the third major group of relations in an econometric model. They represent the free reaction of economic subjects to certain stimuli. An obvious example of this kind of relation is the consumption function. If people have spendable income, they are bound to spend some on consumption but the amount is theirs to decide. The residual error in a reaction equation represents among other things, the fact that people are free to do what they like. However, in any reaction equation, there will almost certainly be a systematic remainder element in the residual error because the list of stimuli is bound to be incomplete. This is particularly true of the rather crude consumption function as shown in (1.3.ex.3). Factors such as the availability of consumer credit, the age distribution of the existing stock of durable goods and the presence of debts, are bound to influence consumption. Furthermore, not all stimuli are suitable for statistical measurement. A rumour that there may be war in the near future will send people to the shops to hoard and subsequently when the rumour has subsided, we will find that consumption in that particular year is in excess of what we should otherwise expect. This extra-consumption cannot be said to be an unexplained residual as we know perfectly well why people bought more than they would have done otherwise. But we cannot measure the intensity of the rumour and as a consequence we are not in a position to predict people's behaviour if and when a new rumour develops.

Technical relations. The obvious example of a technical relation in an econometric model is a production function. In the example in the previous section, there are no purely technical relations, but a production function is assumed to be behind the demand-function for investment.

11

Investment is a meaningful response to an increase in the level of production, only because investment increases production-capacity; but for a production function, (1.3.ex.4) has the time lag the wrong way round. Technically, production increases after there has been investment and this is termed a 'gestation lag'. However, according to (1.3.ex.4), production can increase first, and afterwards this results in investment. This makes it into a reaction equation because the term $2(p_{t-1}-p_{t-2})$ represents entrepreneural reaction to the stimulus of increased production.

1.5. THE NATURE OF STOCHASTIC RELATIONS

The computational procedure of ordinary least squares correlation is assumed known with the reader. This section has been written in order to warn him against a too uncritical use of the results of estimating-algorithms and to this end therefore we briefly summarise the assumptions underlying the statistical model. Firstly, we have the very concept of what a stochastic relation is. The stochastic relation consists of a compound of an exact relationship and a random error term. We have no direct observations of the error and as a result the true values of the parameters cannot be known precisely. They must be estimated approximately, by minimizing a measure of the sample residuals, relative to assumed values of the regression coefficients. With regard to the error; the standard assumption here is that it is normally distributed. This normality assumption is based on application[5] of the *central limit theorem*, by which the sum of a large number of mutually independent variables is normally distributed, provided that none of the individual variables is dominant in the sum. Both these assumptions are highly dubious in practice. The first assumption may be true for institutional relations, as long as the institutional arrangements remain the same, and for technical relations, as long as there is no change in technology. It is almost certainly untrue for reaction equations because the reaction of economic subjects is conditioned by attitudes which are part of the cultural pattern of their society. It is known that such attitudes do change over time and that these changes in attitudes towards economic behaviour are not in themselves measurable. In addition they cannot be verified objectively, as is the case with fiscal and monetary regulations.

They do however influence the measurable data in a systematic way, contrary to what the statistical model assumes. The second assumption, the assumed absence of major single factors in the error, is even more doubtful. For example, in Section 1.4, we mentioned the influence of a rumour of possible war on consumer behaviour. Some of the above-mentioned restrictive assumptions can [6] in fact be relaxed although this may, or may not, lead to somewhat different estimates for the economic parameters. However, *any* formalised model has to assume the absence of any systematic influence outside the formal model and for this reason one is bound to be on dubious ground. The use of least squares and related methods for estimating models can be defended, in spite of the above criticism of the underlying statistical model(s). The reasoning is simple, and is as follows: Numerical values for the coefficients of the economic model have to be obtained by some means or other. One would then prefer small unexplained residuals relative to large ones, but the true confidence intervals of the resulting relationship, are wider than one would infer from the statistical model.

1.6. INSTRUMENTS, TARGET-VARIABLES AND DATA[7]

Exogenous variables can be classified into two groups: instruments and data. The difference is subjective, more precisely, the point of view of a particular policy-maker. Instruments are the variables under the direct control of the authorities. In fact, within a government bureaucracy different ministries or their departments control different instruments. One of the principal functions of a planning organization will then be, to advise the authorities as to what levels of the different instruments might be appropriate for the attainment of an agreed policy.

In the example-model in Section 3, the variable 'tax free minimum' is an obvious example of an instrument. On the other hand, there are the policy-aims. One way of formulating the policy-aims is by specifying certain specific targets, such as 'equilibrium balance of payments', 'full employment' etc. These are specified values of certain of the jointly dependent variables and the policy-maker will *require* these target-variables to attain certain values. The role of the economic planner is to find if possible, a set of values of the instruments, by which one can expect the target-values to be attained and in this connection the planner will have to consider the second group of exogenous variables, the *data*, or data-variables.

13

Data are exogenous variables outside the control of the policy-maker. Under this common heading come different types of variables, as follows: past-values of jointly dependent variables, which cannot be altered now, but have a lagged result on the present, external factors including economic conditions in foreign countries, variables in control of other policy-makers, and climatic factors; variables related to the system, for which no satisfactory fit to a linear relation has been found. The same variable may come in each group, depending on the circumstances. Consider as an example the level of wages and salaries. If there is a centrally controlled incomes-policy, it will be an instrument and the government will be in a position to influence the level of incomes, in order to attain its policy-targets. If however there is a completely free labour market, the level of wages will be an endogenous variable, depending on such factors as profitability and the level of unemployment. Again if there is collective bargaining without interference by the government, then from the government's point of view, the outcome of such bargaining is a datum.

1.7. THE CONDITIONAL FORECAST

Considering once more the illustrative model, described in Section 1.3. Let figures for the exogenous variables be available to the planner as follows:

$$g_t = 20$$
$$tfm_t = 60$$
$$iau_t = 5$$
$$p_{t-1} = 140$$
$$p_{t-2} = 130$$

It is additionally assumed that these figures refer to a future time-period. On substituting these in (1.3.ex.1) until (1.3.ex.4) one obtains:

$$p_t = c_t + i_t + 20 \qquad (1.7.\text{ex}.1)$$

$$si_t = 0.75p_t + 15 \qquad (1.7.\text{ex}.2)$$

$$c_t = 0.80si_t \qquad (1.7.\text{ex}.3)$$

$$i_t = 25 \qquad (1.7.\text{ex}.4)$$

14

Substitute for i_t as 25 and for c_t as 0.80 si_t into (1.7.ex.1) to obtain:

$$p_t = 0.80si_t + 45$$

It is now easy to solve the system as:

$$p_t = 142\tfrac{1}{2}$$

$$si_t = 121\tfrac{7}{8}$$

$$c_t = 97\tfrac{1}{2}$$

$$i_t = 25$$

This forecast is true, relative to two groups of conditions:

(a) That the model is true; and (b) That the assumed values of the exogenous variables will be realised.

The first condition is obvious, but particularly unhelpful, once we consider seriously the possibility of its non-fulfilment. The last condition is more helpful even when considering its non-fulfilment as it enables the political policy-maker to obtain a collection of conditional forecasts, relative to different assumptions about the exogenous variables. Under this heading will come first of all different assumptions about the *instruments* where the planner can forecast the results of alternative policy-decisions. If different assumptions about data may be considered as well then one admits uncertainty about the data, and studies the results of a number of possibilities.

1.8. THE REDUCED FORM

An expression of the dependent variables in terms of the exogenous ones, may be obtained from (1.3.1). On pre-multiplication of (1.3.1) with A^{-1} one obtains:

$$\mathbf{y} = A^{-1} B\mathbf{x} \qquad\qquad (1.8.1)$$

The relation (1.8.1) is known as the *reduced form*[8] of (1.3.1). In our example from Section 1.3, the reduced form is obtained by eliminating p_t from the second equation; c_t from the first, and si_t from the third, and i_t from the first equation.

One obtains:

$$p_t = 2{,}500g_t + 0{,}500tfm_t + 2{,}500iau_t + 5{,}000p_{t-1} - 5{,}000p_{t-2}$$
$$si_t = 1{,}875g_t + 0{,}625tfm_t + 1{,}875iau_t + 3{,}750p_{t-1} - 3{,}750p_{t-2}$$
$$c_t = 1{,}500g_t + 0{,}500tfm_t + 1{,}500iau_t + 3{,}000p_{t-1} - 3{,}000p_{t-2}$$
$$i_t = \qquad\qquad\qquad\qquad\quad 1{,}000iau_t + 2{,}000p_{t-1} - 2{,}000p_{t-2}$$

The reduced form can be used to generate a whole family of alternative forecasts.

Once the reduced form has been computed, a forecast is obtained by post-multiplying $A^{-1}B$ with the assumed vector of exogenous variables. The forecast discussed in Section 1.7, is of course one of them.

$$\begin{bmatrix} 2{,}500 & 0{,}500 & 2{,}500 & 5{,}000 & -5{,}000 \\ 1{,}875 & 0{,}625 & 1{,}875 & 3{,}750 & -3{,}750 \\ 1{,}500 & 0{,}500 & 1{,}500 & 3{,}000 & -3{,}000 \\ & & 1{,}000 & 2{,}000 & -2{,}000 \end{bmatrix} \begin{bmatrix} 20 \\ 60 \\ 5 \\ 140 \\ 130 \end{bmatrix} = \begin{bmatrix} 142{,}500 \\ 121{,}875 \\ 97{,}500 \\ 25{,}000 \end{bmatrix}$$

But now consider a proposal that government expenditure on goods and services be limited to only 19 units, instead of 20 as originally considered.

The new conditional forecast is obtained without renewed reference to the equation system as such. Instead, simply subtract the first column of the reduced form from the old forecast to obtain:

$$\begin{bmatrix} p_t \\ si_t \\ c_t \\ i_t \end{bmatrix} (\text{new}) = \begin{bmatrix} 142{,}500 \\ 121{,}875 \\ 97{,}500 \\ 25{,}000 \end{bmatrix} - \begin{bmatrix} 2{,}500 \\ 1{,}875 \\ 1{,}500 \\ - \end{bmatrix} = \begin{bmatrix} 140 \\ 120 \\ 96 \\ 25 \end{bmatrix}$$

This amounts to a computation of the difference between the old and the new forecast, by post-multiplying the reduced form with the difference of the two vectors of exogenous variables.

1.9. SUBSYSTEMS

We may define a subsystem, by a suitable partitioning of

$$A\mathbf{y} = B\mathbf{x} \qquad\qquad\qquad (1.3.1)$$

16

and its matrices

$$A = \begin{bmatrix} A_{11} & A_{12} \\ A_{21} & A_{22} \end{bmatrix} \tag{1.9.1}$$

should be partitioned in such a way that A_{11} is square and non-singular, and

$$B = \begin{bmatrix} B'_1 \\ B'_2 \end{bmatrix} \tag{1.9.2}$$

should be partitioned so that B'_1 has the same number of rows as

$$A'_1 = [A_{11} \quad A_{12}] \tag{1.9.3}$$

The purpose of the partitioning is to define a system of lower order

$$A_{11}\, \mathbf{y}_1 = B'_1 \mathbf{x} - A_{12}\, \mathbf{y}_2 \tag{1.9.4}$$

which is the first block-row of (1.3.1.) but now treating $\mathbf{y}_2$ as exogenous.

The concept of a subsystem may arise in two ways. We may have a model with a composite structure, which consists of several models as subsystems, each of them being a full model in its own right. An example of this type of subsystem would be a world-trade model, built up out of a number of national models. But within the context of a single-economy model, a subsystem may also refer to a particular *mechanism*, a particular bit of economic theory.

Example
Consider again the model discussed in Section 1.3. We now treat *investment* as exogenous and then of course drop the investment equation. We then have a 'consumption subsystem' which is in fact the Keynesian (Keynes [31], Chapter 10) *multiplier model*, as follows:

p_t	si_t	c_t	=	i_t	g_t	tfm_t
1.00	–	– 1.00		1.00	1.00	–
– 0.75	1.00	–		–	–	0.25
–	– 0.80	1.00		–	–	–

17

The partitioning of A and B will now be obvious:

$$
\begin{array}{cccc}
p_t & si_t & c_t & i_t \\
\end{array}
$$

$$
\left[
\begin{array}{ccc|c}
1.00 & - & -\,1.00 & -\,1.00 \\
-\,0.75 & 1.00 & - & - \\
- & -\,0.80 & 1.00 & - \\
\hline
- & - & - & 1.00 \\
\end{array}
\right] \quad \text{for} \quad A
$$

and

$$
\begin{array}{ccccc}
g_t & tfm_t & iau_t & p_{t-1} & p_{t-2} \\
\end{array}
$$

$$
\left[
\begin{array}{ccccc}
1.00 & - & - & - & - \\
- & 0.25 & - & - & - \\
- & - & - & - & - \\
\hline
- & - & 1.00 & 2.00 & -\,2.00 \\
\end{array}
\right] \quad \text{for} \quad B
$$

From the formal structure of the model, it appears that the investment-equation alone also satisfies the definition of a sub-system. (One can reorder the system making investment the first variable and the investment equation the first equation.) We may then say that this model contains two subsystems, a consumption-multiplier subsystem, and an investment subsystem, which is an accelerator-mechanism. The concept of a multiplier mechanism may be widened to any subsystem which explains a final demand category (consumption, but also possibly investment) as a certain fraction of income, at the same time giving rise to income. In this connection I propose the more general term 'expenditure multiplier'. The investment subsystem has the peculiar property that one unit of extra production in the period t will generate more than one unit of demand for investment-goods in the next period. This may obviously give rise to a cumulative process, since investment goods must be produced. For this reason this particular type of subsystem is known as an *accelerator mechanism*.

The combination of the two subsystems into one model may be described verbally by saying that the model contains the Keynesian multiplier mechanism and an accelerator mechanism. Of course the two mechanisms (subsystems) form one model, and we will get multiplier effects of the demand for investment goods generated by the accelerator mechanism. Additional investment will be accompanied by more consumption as well, because it generates production and income and this will again have its feedback on the demand for investment-goods in the next period.

The combination of the two mechanisms into one model is not just a question of having the effects of both mechanisms side by side; they influence each other. In this example, the inter-relationship is a one-sided one. The investment influences the rest of the model, but the current level of investment is not itself influenced by the current values of the other variables. This is reflected in the structure of the coefficients-matrix in the fact that A_{21} is a zero matrix. There is of course no requirement that this should be so, although it happens not infrequently.

NOTES TO CHAPTER I

[1] Recommended reading for those not familiar with matrix algebra: Fuller [19] *or* (more elementary) Cohn [14].
[2] This convention follows first of all the Dutch Central Planning Bureau's tradition, and also Christ [13].
[3] Only lower case is used, because the whole model is in constant prices.
[4] This classification closely follows the Dutch publication *Centraal Economisch Plan 1955* [5] and has been generally accepted ever since.
[5] In this connection, see Christ [13], p. 142–143.
[6] Recommended to read for those not familiar with least square regression: Goldberger [20], Chapters 4, 5 and 7.
[7] To my knowledge this terminology is due to Tinbergen [56].
[8] This term is Goldberger's [21].

CHAPTER II

THE SHORT-TERM FORECASTING MODEL

2.1. WHAT IS 'SHORT-TERM'?

The short-term forecasting model is the first of a series of types of models, to be discussed in some of the following chapters. In fact the term '*annual* macro-economic model' would be more appropriate. The one essentially different feature of quarterly models, seasonal adjustment, is not discussed in this book. This type of model is the oldest kind of model in existence, and up to now it is also probably the one that is most frequently applied in practice, mainly for macro-economic policy-decisions. The essential short-term element is the assumption that demand is always met by supply. This type of model is essentially a *demand* model. An increase in demand will have certain side-effects such as higher prices, increased imports, etcetera, but a realistic short-term model should not identify[1] potential production with sold output.

2.2. AN EXAMPLE OF A SHORT-TERM MODEL

We will now discuss a particular example of a short-term forecasting model which substantially, is the model published[2] by the Dutch Central Planning Bureau in 1955. A number of alterations have been made to the model by the present author. Some of these alterations are simply a matter of presentation and some are of substance. The changes in the presentation are the following:

First of all the names of the variables have been changed, so as to correspond to abbreviations of the *English* words describing them. The system of notation is by and large the same in the original where the letters refer to Dutch words. Secondly, the variable 'investment' has been changed to mean *gross* investment; in the original a number of relations contain the addition of (net) investment and depreciation. Thirdly, the basic account of production (the balance equation) has been re-formulated, making a number of value-variables and their definitions redundant. Fourthly, the institutional relations defining direct taxation have been reformulated in terms of spendable income-flows, rather than tax-flows as this leads to a considerable simplification of the consumption function.

There are also some alterations in the substance of the model, to be discussed below in conjunction with the equation in question. The purpose of these alterations is not only a question of the preferability of a particular type of relation, but also to familiarize the reader with the kind of arguments involved in the pros and cons of particular specifications. The model is formulated in terms *increments*, the chief advantage of which is the elimination of a large number of constant terms. The remaining constants now represent either changes in the exogenous variables or time-trends. In a number of relations, the levels occur as parameters and these will be indicated with the same symbol, with a bar. This is similar to the original.

The model can now be described as follows:

List of variables (with some assumed initial values)

Value	(Type)	Price	(Type)	Quantity	(Type)	of....
L	(end) 8,900	w	(exo) 1,000	l	(end) 8,900	employed labour
				lf	(exo) 8,900	labour-force, as given exogenous
C	(end) 10,000	pc	(end) 1,000	c	(end) 10,000	consumption
IV	6,000	pivg	(end) 1,000	iv	(end) 6,000	investment by enterprises
		see above		giv	(exo) 2,000	government and semi-public investment
		pst	(end) 1,000	st	(end) 0,500	stock-accumulation
		w	(exo) (see above with labour	gl	(exo) 1,000	government labour (salaries)
E	(end) 5,000	pex	(end) 1,000	e	(end) 5,000	exports
IM	(end) 7,321	pim	(exo) 1,000	im	(end) 7,321	imports
P	(end)					profits (gross, before direct tax)

Value	(Type)	Price	(Type)	Quantity	(Type)	of ....
SL	(end)					spendable labour-income
SP	(end)					spendable profit-income
IT	(end) 1,319	*ITAU*	(exo) 1,319			indirect taxes net of subsidies
LTAU	(exo)					autonomous (change) in tax on labour
PTAU	(exo)					autonomous (change) in tax on profit
D	(exo)					depreciation
		pcfp	(exo)			competing foreign production
				riv	(exo)	investment for re-placement

The variables, as occurring in the model, are the *increments* in the current periods value relative to the levels of the previous period. Levels of previous periods will be indicated with a bar above the corresponding symbol. The explicit mentioning of the time index *t* is suppressed and where lagged variables do occur, these will be indicated simply by means of an index −1. The increments, by contrast, will be indicated with a prime.

The equations
Definition identities

$$(1) \qquad L' = l' + 8{,}90w'$$

$$(2) \qquad C' = c' + 10{,}00pc'$$

$$(3) \qquad E' = e' + 5{,}00pe'$$

$$(4) \qquad IM' = im' + 7{,}32pim'$$

$$(5) \qquad P' = C' + iv' + giv' + gl' + st' + E' - IM' \\ + 8{,}00pgiv' + 1{,}00w' + 0{,}50pst' - L' - IT' - D'$$

Institutional relations

$$(6) \qquad SL' = 0{,}80L' + 0{,}40\,(lf' - l') - LTAU'$$

$$(7) \qquad SP' = 0{,}50P' \qquad\qquad - PTAU'$$

$$(8) \qquad IT' = 0{,}04IM' + 0{,}05C' \qquad + ITAU'$$

Technical relations

(9) $im' = 1{,}1\,(0{,}23c' + 0{,}32iv' + 0{,}32'giv' + 0{,}45e' + 0{,}59st')$

(10) $l' = 0{,}4\,(0{,}40c' + 0{,}35iv' + 0{,}20exp' + 0{,}188st') + lg'$

Reaction equations

(11) $C' = 0{,}85SL + 0{,}40SP'$

(12) $iv' = 0{,}75\,(c' + iv' + giv' + st' + e' - im')_{-1} - 0{,}3\overline{iv} + riv'$

(13) $st' = 0{,}20\,(c' + iv' + giv' + st' + e' - im') - 0{,}60\overline{st}$

(14) $e' = 2{,}50\,(pcfp' - pex')$

Price equations

(15) $pc' = \tfrac{2}{3}\,(0{,}23pim' + 0{,}075\,\dfrac{ITAU'}{1{,}32} + 0{,}40w') - 0{,}02$

(16) $pivg' = \tfrac{2}{3}\,(0{,}32pim' + 0{,}04\,\dfrac{ITAU'}{1{,}32} + 0{,}35w') - 0{,}02$

(17) $pst' = \tfrac{2}{3}\,(0{,}59pim' + 0{,}08\,\dfrac{ITAU'}{1{,}32} + 0{,}18w') - 0{,}02$

(18) $pe' = \tfrac{1}{2}\,(0{,}45pim' + 0{,}05\,\dfrac{ITAU'}{1{,}32} + 0{,}20w') - 0{,}01 + \tfrac{1}{2}\,pcfp'$

2.3. LINEAR APPROXIMATION

The model described in the previous section is linear, only by approximation, whereas the true model is non-linear. This non-linearity arises from the well known relation

Value = price × quantity

For example, if we consider labour the true relation is

$$\bar{L} + L' = (\bar{w} + w')\,(\bar{l} + l') \qquad (2.3.\text{ex}.1)$$

The (new) level of the value is the (new) level of the price, multiplied by the (new) level of the quantity. In a similar way, we will have for the old level

$$\bar{L} = \bar{w} \cdot \bar{l} \qquad (2.3.\text{ex}.2)$$

23

by (2.3.ex.1), we obtain (multiply out the right-hand side)

$$\bar{L} + L' = \bar{w}\bar{l} + \bar{w}l' + \bar{l}w' + w'l' \tag{2.3.ex.3}$$

By (2.3.ex.2), this reduces to

$$L' = \bar{w}l' + \bar{l}w' + w'l' \tag{2.3.ex.4}$$

We can now evaluate $\bar{w}$ and $\bar{l}$, for the particular initial conditions assumed; $\bar{w} = 1,000$; $\bar{l} = 8,90$ to give

$$L' = l' + 8,90w' + w'l' \tag{2.3.ex.5}$$

Now consider a particular set of values for w and l. For example a 6% rise in the wage-rate and a 1.1% rise in employment

$$w' = 0,06; \quad l' = 0,10$$

The increment in the wage-sum is then evaluated by (2.3.ex.5) as

$$L' = 0,100 + 0,534 + 0,006 \tag{2.3.ex.6}$$

It is immediately evident that no great error is made by counting only the linear terms in (2.3.ex.4). The quadratic term is the *product* of two small numbers, which we can suppress. The outcome is dominated by the linear terms. The approximation is however valid only over a limited interval. If we should consider a doubling of both price and quantity, then the value would be increased four-fold, while for the linear approximation the increase would be three-fold. In our example of 6% and 1.1% the error is less than one hundredth *of the total variation.*

Generally one may approximate a not too strongly non-linear differentiable function, as follows: First, formulate the functional relation in such a way that both sides of the equation can be differentiated without undue complication. Then obtain the partial derivatives of both sides of the equation, relative to all variables, and equate the total differentials of the two sides of the equation

$$\sum_{j=1}^{n} \frac{\partial \text{ left}}{\partial v_j} dv_j = \sum_{j=1}^{n} \frac{\partial \text{ right}}{\partial v_j} dv_j \tag{2.3.1}$$

where the symbol 'left' indicates the left-hand side of the original relation, the symbol 'right' the right-hand side and v_j the jth variable, there being n variables.

In our example, this would correspond to

$$dL = w \, dl + l \, dw. \qquad\qquad (2.3.ex.7)$$

Then obtain a consistent set of figures, satisfying the original non-linear relation, at a point not too far away from the expected solution. In the example, these were supplied by the base-year data.

Now substitute the numerical evaluation of the partial derivatives, for the expressions of the partial derivatives themselves.

Hence, in the neighbourhood of the known solution, we will have for

$$w = 1{,}000 \quad \text{and} \quad l = 8{,}90$$

$$dL = dl + 8{,}90 \, dw \qquad\qquad (2.3.ex.8)$$

The approximation will then arise, because one extends (2.3.ex.8) which is strictly correct only for infinitely small differences, to finite differences, to obtain:

$$L' = l' + 8{,}90w' \qquad\qquad (2.3.ex.9)$$

2.4. PRODUCTION, INCOME AND ITS DISTRIBUTION

A correct set of accounting identities is the basic framework of any econometric model of this kind. In this respect there is first of all:

$$L + P + IT - FFA =$$
$$C + IV + GIV + ST + GL - D + E - IM \qquad (2.4.1)$$

This is the familiar[3] accounting balance, linking production to expenditure after correcting for exports and imports. Most of the value-variables in (2.4.1) are in the model; but some only in volume. One variable is not considered in the model at all, namely FFA (Factor-income From Abroad). On this point the model is, in fact, in error because it does not acknowledge this particular accounting variable. The assumption is that this variable is exogenous and is expected to be invariant with the consequence that it would be eliminated from the model, which is measured in terms of increments. Economic equations systems have followed the

25

development of National Accounting. In the thirties many writers[4] simply wrote

$$Y \equiv C + I,$$

where Y was both production and income and the two were supposed to be identical to consumption plus investment. Excluding factor-incomes from abroad the accounting-balance is the fifth equation of the model.

The variables IV, GIV, GL and ST are not in the model, but have been replaced by the corresponding functions of quantity and price. By assumption[5] investment by enterprises, public and semi-public investment have the same price, giving rise to the combination of $\overline{iv} \cdot pgiv + \overline{giv} \cdot pgiv$ into a single term $(6+2)$ $pgiv = 8pgiv$. The *volume* of production is in the model by Equations (12) and (13) for investment and stockbuilding, as $c + iv + giv + st + e - im$. This is production of the 'enterprises' sector. The salaries of public servants have been excluded, since they are not complementary to either capital goods or inventories. The specific way in which the accounting identities are brought into the equations system, is of course, arbitrary. The balance may be written just as well in volume, instead of in values as we did above. The particular collection of variables which is defined explicitly both in volume and in value is also somewhat arbitrary[6]. *The distribution* of the income is largely governed by the relative increases in production and employment. The price-structure is in fact fully exogenous and furthermore, production and employment are related to each other. The result is that income distribution is a corollary of the levels of activity. Since the elasticity of employment relative to production is less than unity, high activity will result in a low share for labour, and vice versa. One could of course counteract such a result by variation in the (exogenous) wage rate.

2.5. THE INSTITUTIONAL RELATIONS

Relations (6)–(8) are quite straightforward and require little explanation. For labour, there is a 20% marginal rate of taxation, and a redundancy benefit for unemployed labour, at a rate of 40% of the income of employed labour.

The constant $LTAU'$ represents an autonomous *change* in the fiscal regulations. Relative to (1.3.ex.2) the difference is that this model is in terms of increments, whereas the one in Chapter I is in levels. The *level* of the tax-free minimum is automatically eliminated when estimating in increments. Income from profit is taxed rather heavier at a marginal rate of 50%; leaving in effect a marginal spendable rate of 50%. Indirect taxes are specified as a basic import duty of 4% and in addition a purchase tax of 5% on average, chargeable only on consumption. In fact, of course, fiscal regulations may be fairly complicated, and one may have to resort to regression analysis in order to establish the values of the coefficients.

2.6. THE DEMAND FOR PRODUCTION FACTORS

The next five equations are the econometric core of any short-term forecasting model. They describe what will happen to the demand for production factors (imports and labour), and final output flows (consumption, investment and inventories) given certain changes in prices, income, taxes, etcetera. The distinction between 'technical relations' and 'reaction equations' in fact means this: For imports and labour, the constructors of the model were excluding any dynamic analysis, the demand for import and labour being directly linked to current output.

The coefficients before the brackets in (9) and (10) represent a transformation from average to marginal factor output ratios. The expression within the brackets is assumed[7] to be the demand function for the production factor in question, corresponding to the input-output model. The actual increment in factor demand is then regressed on the theoretical increment in demand as computed by means of the input-output model. The order of magnitude of the elasticities is the same as in the original model[8].

2.7. THE CONSUMPTION FUNCTION

This is a pure reaction equation and in the present model is a very simple function. Marginal expenditure quotes of spendable income are listed as 85% of income from labour and 40% of income attributable to profits. More complicated functions can and have been specified in later models. The consumption function of the Klein-Goldberger model contains an autoregressive term $0.23 c_{t-1}$; the Central Planning Bureau's 1961 model considers lagged influences of the previous period income as well as a separate treatment of volume and price. These are only some of the possible refinements that could be brought into the model. Unfortunately, further improvements in the consumption function are unlikely to result in a substantially better forecasting record. The reason is simple; the greater part[9] of the error in forecasting consumption is already due to poor forecast of the determinants of consumption: incomes and prices.

2.8. THE DEMAND FOR INVESTMENT GOODS

The general type of investment function incorporated in this particular model is known as a 'flexible accelerator'. A *fixed* accelerator would mean a relation of the type

$$i_t = \kappa (p_{t-1} - p_{t-2}) \tag{2.8.1}$$

or, without the time-lag[10]

$$i_t = \kappa (p_t - p_{t-1}) \tag{2.8.2}$$

It is assumed that entrepreneurs adjust their capacity to output to the full extent of any increase in output. The coefficient κ is assumed to be a technical parameter and in order to increase production capacity by one unit it is necessary to invest κ units. At any point in time, output and capacity may of course be different from each other. This involves a non-observed variable 'production capacity'.

$$i_t = \kappa (ca_{t+1} - ca_t) \tag{2.8.3}$$

The assumption that capacity is at once restored to the full extent may in practice be too rigid. A more flexible entrepreneurial behaviour assumes:

$$i_t = \alpha \cdot \kappa (p_{t-1} + \beta - ca_t) \tag{2.8.4}$$

This relation[11] involves the current year's capacity and the previous year's output. The reasoning behind this type of relation is as follows: Consider in the first place the entrepreneurial decision on the current year's investment, presumably this decision is finally taken somewhere towards the end of the previous year. At that moment the production capacity of the current (then still future) year will be known on the basis of what is then being invested, but output is only known for the previous (i.e. then current) year. Entrepreneurs by assumption attempt to maintain capacity in excess of output to the amount of β.

On any 'excess demand'

$$ed_t = p_{t-1} + \beta - ca_t \tag{2.8.5}$$

they will react by investing and will plan an increase in capacity equal to a fraction α of the excess demand. On the assumption that this reaction is effective in the next period one obtains (2.8.4). Fortunately the unobserved variable 'capacity' can be eliminated and the parameters estimated; even the constant β can be eliminated. To this end ca_t is solved out of (2.8.4) to give:

$$\kappa \cdot ca_t = \kappa \left(p_{t-1} + \beta \right) - \frac{1}{\alpha} i_t \tag{2.8.6}$$

On evaluating (2.8.3) by substitution for the capacity by (2.8.6) we obtain

$$i_t = \kappa \left(p_t - p_{t-1} \right) - \frac{1}{\alpha} \left(i_{t+1} - i_t \right) \tag{2.8.7}$$

Solve (2.8.7) for $i_{t+1} - i_t$, and reduce the time index with one unit

$$i_t - i_{t-1} = \alpha\kappa \left(p_{t-1} - p_{t-2} \right) - \alpha i_{t-1} \tag{2.8.8}$$

We can now use the notation of increments and levels (as used in the model as such) and suppress the explicit writing of the time indices

$$i' = \alpha\kappa p'_{-1} - \alpha l \tag{2.8.9}$$

Apart from the fact that numerical values of the coefficients have been filled in, this is the twelfth equation of the model for *new* investment, a term for replacement is then added exogenously. The above equation is different from the one in the actual 1955 C.P.B. model in as much that the latter model did not contain the lag in the variable p'. Framed in the present notation as used for (2.8.9) it would read:

$$i' = 0.25 \, p' - 0.10 \, l \tag{2.8.10}$$

Leaving aside theoretical considerations about the proper time lag, the order of magnitude of the coefficients in the 1955 model is somewhat unrealistic. The coefficient for l would mean in effect that planned capacity is adjusted towards a realized output by only 10% in any year and this is on the very low side indeed. One rather suspects that 0.25 simply represents the fact that investment itself is about 25% of the output. The

29

present equation does not include any financial factors and probably the proper approach here is to use a combination of capacity output influences of an accelerator type based on lagged variables of one period and upwards; together with financial effects reflecting the 'pruning' of investment projects, based on the more recent financial position. Profits and the supply of liquidity would come under this heading. Equations of such a mixed type can and have been specified and estimated (See Van den Beld [3]).

2.9. THE DEMAND FOR INVENTORIES

The equation for stock formation is a flexible accelerator of the same type as used for investment in fixed assets with one main difference. For inventories, it is not unreasonable that some degree of adaptation of the level of stocks to the level of output is effective in the current period. The coefficients as estimated by the C.P.B. imply an equilibrium stock-output ratio of $0.20:0.60=0.33$ and an adjustment fraction in any period of 60%. These coefficients are not unreasonable in their magnitudes. Later models have considered financial factors in addition to a pure flexible accelerator.

2.10. THE PRICE EQUATIONS

The price equations have been set aside from the reaction equations. The reason is that they describe an assumed reaction under rather restrictive a priori assumptions. Internal prices are purely a function of costs, the wage rate and imports. The expressions within the brackets are based on accounting data (input-output analysis). Estimated is a coefficient of adaptation ($\frac{2}{3}$ in the example) and a trend representing increase in productivity (-2%). It is assumed that this estimate is made for the economy as a whole. The price equation for export is somewhat different and here it is assumed that this price is also influenced by the competing price of foreign production; for a weighting factor of $\frac{1}{2}$ the latter is simply followed. These equations represent a refinement relative to the original model as published by the C.P.B.

2.11. SUPPLY AND DEMAND

In 1955 Tinbergen[12] wrote "It seems desirable to follow some generally accepted system of introducing all these relations in order that a judgement of the set of relations concerning its completeness be easily possible. This might be the beginning of a systematic study of the characteristics of economic models. Such a systematic setup should consist first of all of a list of the markets considered, indicating product markets and factor markets separately. For each of them demand and supply relations should be present." In this connection it is worth mentioning Tinbergen's 1936 model [58]. This is a full-scale short-term forecasting model. In fact it is in some respects more sophisticated than the 1955 model of the C.P.B. discussed above. In particular, it does indeed consider separate relations for the following: consumer goods, investment goods, imports of raw materials, imports of finished investment goods, and imports of finished consumer goods. Investment goods are not considered as exportable and the export of consumer goods [13] is also the total export of goods. By Tinbergen's 1955 criterion as quoted above, one should have *two* volume relations for each good. One relation would give the supply and the other the demand, an endogenous price could be solved between the two. On the face of it it seems that some attempt in this direction was made in 1936 but in actual fact this is not really the case. All the endogenous prices have a price equation on a cost basis, both in the 1936 and in the 1955 model. Both [14] models are logically consistent with Tinbergen's criterion of completeness, albeit as borderline cases.

The *demand* relations for each good are there, but instead of supply relations one can observe either a price equation or else an exogenous price. One has to assume an infinite supply elasticity and, as observed already, this is an essential short-term element. Endogenous prices are explained as functions of exogenous prices, wages, import price and competing export price with the result that the model has a block-triangular structure. The matrix A (the matrix of the coefficients for the dependent variables) can be partitioned in a price block-row and a remainder 15×19 block-row. The price block-row will have unit coefficients on the diagonal and elsewhere only zeros.

2.12. CAPACITY

Attempts towards a more realistic treatment of the supply capacity have been concentrated on the supply of labour and the reasons for this are obvious. The conditional forecast: "Given the proposed tax reduction, there will be as the outcome an unused machine capacity of minus 5 billion dollar output capacity", is nonsense. But that forecast is in effect never made because there are no data on machine capacity. The conditional forecast: "Given the proposed tax reduction, there will be as a result an unemployment of minus one half percent", is just as nonsensical, although quite conceivable with a linear model. Understandably, some attempts have been made to remedy this situation. Following the general notion of market clearing by the price, it is only logical that one has looked at the wage rate as the remedy and this introduces the wage rate as a dependent variable, instead of being an exogenous factor.

The standard approach is to link the increment of the wage rate to the level of unemployment, with or without a suitable lag. There may also be a feedback from the price index of consumption goods. The labour market factor is of course non-linear and this approach has been followed by the Dutch Central Planning Bureau's later models, and by Klein and Goldberger for the United States [28]. The relationship is in fact also listed – but not used operationally – in Tinbergen's 1936 model [58]. This approach cannot be said to be completely successful because wages are both prices and incomes with the result that it is not at all certain that an increase in the wage-rate will in fact reduce employment. Tinbergen's 1936 reduced form gives an *increase* in employment as a result of an increase in the wage rate. The later Dutch models give a fall in employment for an increase in the wage rate. But some of the reasons for this are specific for an open economy. With exports at a level of about ⅔ of domestic production any increase in consumption as a result of higher wages will be more than compensated by a reduction in the volume of exports – due to loss of competitiveness. Should the United States ever experience the kind of super-full employment (excess demand for labour), as experienced in N.W. Europe in the early sixties then the approach is likely to break down.

It is the firm opinion of the present writer that the proper treatment of capacity will have to consider inequalities. Given a certain price and income situation there is a resulting demand for goods (possibly including production factors), which will be satisfied, if and only if, the goods are available.

This would also explain a phenomenon reported by Verdoorn and

Post ([59], pp. 179–198). Under conditions of overfull employment an additional demand impulse may actually *reduce* productivity. The price-mechanism ceases to perform its allocative function effectively.

2.13. BUILT-IN STABILIZERS

A built-in stabilizer is a subsystem, which is there in order to prevent the model, or the real economy, from running off course. An example of an *unstable*[15] model is the example in Chapter I. The combination of a multiplier mechanism and an accelerator relation may lead to a cumulative process, which is of the same nature as the business-cycle in the real world, but possibly much more violent. According to this particular model, one isolated unit of public expenditure is associated (by the multiplier mechanism) with $1\frac{1}{2}$ units of consumption, resulting in a total multiplier of $2\frac{1}{2}$ units in the current period. The combination of such a strong multiplier effect with the accelerator mechanism will result in violent reactions. The most common and best-known stabilizer is the 'leak' into direct taxes. This stabilizer in fact *is* in the model in Chapter I. Without taxes, consumption would be 80% of production, and as a result total production would be five times the rest of production. The fact that of an additional unit of production, only $\frac{3}{4}$ unit becomes spendable income reduces the multiplier from –

$$(1 - 0.80)^{-1} \qquad = 5 \quad \text{to}$$
$$(1 - 0.75 \times 0.80)^{-1} = 2\tfrac{1}{2}$$

The term 'built-in stabilizers' did in fact arise because one assumes that the tax-leak was designed for that purpose, in order to stabilize the real economy.

The next important stabilizer is the import-leak. Consider the following model, which is a variant of the model in Chapter I.

$$p_t = c_t + iv_t + g_t + e_t - im_t$$
$$si_t = 0.75 \, (p_t - tfm_t) + tfm_t$$
$$c_t = 0.80 si_t$$
$$im_t = 0.20 p_t$$

Legenda: as in Chapter I, except for the following alterations:

Investment (period t) = iv_t instead of i_t and
new variables e_t = export and im_t = imports.

Exports are exogenous and for imports there is an import-equation. The increment in production will still be $2\frac{1}{2}$ times the increment in production less the increment in consumption. But this difference is now not identical to exogenous expenditure, but to exogenous expenditure less imports.

$$p' = 2\tfrac{1}{2}\,(p' - c') = 2\tfrac{1}{2}\,(g' - im')$$

since the increment in imports is 20% of the increment in production, we will then have

$$1,50p' = 2.50g'$$

The multiplier has been reduced to only just under 2. Further stabilizing effects may arise from the feedback of the domestic market on exports, in which case we will summarize the import and export effect together as a balance-of-payments leak; and from price-adjustments.

2.14. SUMMARY OF THE SHORT-TERM FORECASTING MODEL

The standard short-term forecasting model will consist of:

(a) A set of definition identities and accounting relationships. These relationships will define the income and other value-flow results of any vector of volumes and prices of the accounting flows in the model.

(b) A set of institutional relationships, defining the relation between spendable income and accounted productive income, for each endogenous group of economic decision-makers which is assumed to react via an expenditure multiplier mechanism.

The public policymaker, the government is not considered as a reacting decision-maker, and hence the public income-flow is not as such a relevant variable for budgetary decisions.

(c) For each product-flow there will either be a price-equation, or a supply relation, or the price should be exogenous.[16]

(d) For each good (final demand category or production factor) there will be a demand function. This demand function will be in volume or in value terms. In either case it determines both of them, the two being interdependent via the rest of the model. For some goods, this demand function may of course have the simple form of the demand being exogenous.

NOTES TO CHAPTER II

[1] I believe this requirement to be related to Wold's causal chain criterion, though not going as far as Wold's (see Wold [62], see also Chapter VII).

[2] *Centraal economisch Plan 1955* [5], p. 110.

[3] Those not familiar with national accounting are recommended to read Stone and Stone [52].

[4] As late as 1950: see Hicks [29], p. 170.

[5] This is not a particularly realistic assumption. Public investment tends to have a larger share of construction, and building costs rise faster than production costs of machinery. But it was felt desirable to keep the model reasonably small.

[6] It will generally be desirable to have imports and exports in value explicitly in the model. The reason is that almost any policy problem will have a balance of payments target.

[7] This is not so in the original model [5]. This is based on time series analysis only. The later 1961 model [8] follows the approach as discussed here. The change in the model was made in order to illustrate the use of accounting data.

[8] The marginal demand for labour is considerably less than the average. This is a common feature of all short-term forecasting models. In all probability, this is related to the absence of a negative constant representing exogenous increase in productivity. Statistical estimates of this constant tend to have the wrong sign because labour is retained in recessions.

[9] In 'Forecast and Realization' [7] the Dutch Central Planning Bureau reports the second order moment of the error to be 38 % of the second order moment of the yearly increment in the volume of consumption. On the other hand, D. van der Werf, in a paper, read at the 1968 European Meeting, reports a consumption function for Germany of a fairly simple type with a correlation coefficient of $\hat{R}^2 = 0.93$ also in terms of increments, and after correction for degrees of freedom. (Regrettably, most published models do not give the correlation coefficients.) Most likely, the fairly satisfactory fit of the consumption function is not a specific German phenomenon. The inference is clear. If the determinants of consumption were known, the (stochastic) error would be only about 7 %; the actual error is about 4 times as much. See Van der Werf [61].

[10] See Chapter I, Section 1.3 (ex. 4).

[11] The general type of this relationship is the C.P.B.'s [5]; the specification is the present author's. The C.P.B. mentions Goodwin [22] and Chenery [11] as references. In fact these are more complicated (non-linear) models. See also Meyer [40] and Glauber [40].

[12] See Tinbergen [56], pp.13–14.

[13] For the Dutch economy in 1936, this was not too much of an oversimplification. Today, it would of course be utterly wrong to make this assumption.

[14] In 1955, Tinbergen was the Director of the Central Planning Bureau, and as such responsible for the 1955 model as well.

[15] For a more formal mathematical treatment of the concept of stability see Chapter VII.

[16] The possibility of an exogenous value, controlled by monetary measures cannot be excluded. In that case the price becomes endogenous.

CHAPTER III

THE (STATIC) INPUT-OUTPUT MODEL

3.1. USE OF THE INPUT-OUTPUT MODEL

The main application of the input-output model is in terms of inter-industry analysis.

There are certain types of question which obviously involve the input-output model. Suppose the government initiates a big building pro-gramme, how will it influence other sectors of the economy, besides the building trade?

But also, there are certain questions where this is not so obvious, but valid all the same.

Suppose the import-duties are reduced by an all-round 25% of their former level, how will it influence the cost-of-living?

Such questions can be analysed by means of the input-output costing model. Furthermore, the input-output accounting framework may be useful in the context of a multi-industry model even if one does not make the restrictive assumptions of the Leontief model.

3.2. THE INPUT-OUTPUT TABLE

An input-output table is a way of recording product-streams in a national economy. It classifies each stream of product according to its origin and according to its destination. A product-flow can be classified by its origin, as coming from one of the sectors of production in the national economy, such as industry, agriculture, mining, trade, etc. or as being a primary production-factor. Everything for which a commercial payment is made, while such a payment is not a credit transaction, is labelled as a product-stream. The trader 'produces' trading services, bringing goods from their primary producer to their buyer. The civil servant 'produces' government services, the police and the army produce security services, because they are paid for it. Primary production factors are: imports, labour (wages and salaries), indirect taxes, and profits. The latter two 'production factors' are again an example of the fact that the mere payment of money is sufficient reason to classify such a flow of money as a product-flow. By this device, the sum of all the (payments to) production factors will always be identical to the total revenue of the sale of the product.

By its *destination*, a product-flow can be classified as being delivered to one of the production-sectors, or as being part of the final output. Final output can be divided up into *final demand categories*. Final demand categories are: consumption by private persons, goods and services used by the government, export, investment by enterprises, and stockformation.

The above classification of both primary production factors and of final demand categories is not necessarily exhaustive. Indeed, most published input-output tables split profits into depreciation and net profits; and government into the government's consumption and investment.

Another question relates the classification of government owned and government controlled enterprises. Here the normal procedure is to classify as 'government' only such economic activities as are everywhere run by the government. Such activities as mining, making steel, etc, are classified with the respective sectors of production, whether this is done by the government, or by private enterprise. Most of these accounting problems are in fact not problems of input-output tables, but of national accounting in general.

TABLE II

	1 ind	2 n.i.	3 1–2	4 con	5 gov	6 exp	7 inv	8 sto	9 4–8	10 Total
1 Industry	40	20	60	50	20	130	50	− 10	240	300
2 Non-industry	45	45	90	115	23	50	20	2	210	300
3 Add 1–2	85	65	150	165	43	180	70	− 8	450	600
4 Imports	50	30	80	40	10	–	20	− 10	60	140
5 Net indirect taxes	30	30	60	–	–	–	–	–	–	60
6 Wages	100	120	220	–	80	–	–	–	80	300
7 Gross profits	35	55	90	–	–	–	–	–	–	90
8 Add 4–7	215	235	450	40	90	–	20	− 10	140	590
10 Total	300	300	600	205	133	180	90	− 18	590	–

In the numerical example, given on page 37, the figures have been invented, for the purpose of illustration, We will consider only two sectors, while in fact any published input-output table will have more sectors. We will name the two sectors 'Industry' and 'Non-industry'. The table might then be as Table II (previous page).

The top left-hand block are named the *inter-industry deliveries*. They consist of such things as steel delivered to the shipbuilding industry (row industry, column industry), or fertilizer delivered to agriculture (row industry, column non-industry). Each row gives a complete account of where the product is going. Each column gives a complete account of from where the product flows come (=who is getting the money).

Part of the primary production factors go directly into final demand. There is direct use of imports for private consumption, by the government, as investment goods, and stockpiling (depletion) of imported goods. There is also direct use of labour by the government.

3.3. THE INPUT-OUTPUT PRODUCTION MODEL

The basic assumption of the input-output production model is one of *fixed proportionality*, the required use of raw materials and semi-finished goods being proportional to the level of production. Each sector of production is seen as a production process, which must for one unit of output, consume a certain vector of inputs. By assumption, we have

$$x_{ij} = a_{ij} t_j \tag{3.3.1}$$

Here, x_{ij} is the output flow of sector i, ($i=1, 2...n$), delivered to sector j, for the purpose of being consumed as input into sector j ($j=1, 2...n$). For $i=n+1,..., n+m$, the interpretation is the same, x_{ij} is the consumption of the ith good, which is a non-produced good, a primary production factor, by sector j. t_j is the total output level of the jth sector. The a_{ij} are the 'input-output coefficients'. They are obtained by dividing the entries in the input-output table, through their column total.

$$a_{ij} = x_{ij} : t_j \tag{3.3.2}$$

If (3.3.1) is seen as a stochastic relation, the minimally required number of observations for its estimation by ordinary least squares is just one, the same as the number of parameters.

It is common practice to estimate input-output models on the basis of just one input-output table, using the most recent one available. In our example we would have for instance:

$$a_{12} = 20:300 = 0.066$$

Hence we would assume

$$x_{1,2} = 0.066t_2$$

This relation is generalized to an arbitrary level of the total output. Balance equations of the first two sectors of production will then give rise to the following system of linear equations:

$$t_1 = 0.133t_1 + 0.066t_2 + f_1$$
$$t_2 = 0.150t_1 + 0.150t_2 + f_2$$
(3.3.ex.1)

where t_1 and t_2 are the total outputs of sectors 1 and 2 and f_1 and f_2 the final outputs.

Similarly for the four primary income categories: for imports

$$y_1 = .167t_1 + .100t_2 + h_1$$
(3.3.ex.2)

Here y_1 is the total requirement of the first production factor, and h_1 is the direct final use of the first production factor.

We will make the same constant proportionality assumption about indirect taxes as for production factors, not for technical but for institutional reasons. At constant prices, the same relation for profits would of course hold as well and it would not always be necessary to add it explicitly, since the other relations already specify that costs are a fixed proportion of output. If a profits-row were added it would define total profit. Such an 'input-output' relation would then be equivalent to a macroeconomic relation for profits. We can then write the system (3.3.ex.1) as

$$\left. \begin{array}{l} ,867t_1 - ,066t_2 = f_1 \\ - ,150t_1 + ,850t_2 = f_2 \end{array} \right\}$$
(3.3.ex.3)

and we can solve for t_1 and t_2 in terms of f_1 and f_2

$$\left. \begin{array}{l} t_1 = 1,169f_1 + ,091f_2 \\ t_2 = ,206f_1 + 1,192f_2 \end{array} \right\}$$
(3.3.ex.4)

The interpretation is as follows: The levels of total production of the two sectors are named as variables, t_1 and t_2. The total production of the two sectors is then solved in terms of the final demand for their products, f_1 and f_2.

(3.3.ex.4) is the reduced form of (3.3.ex.3)

Input-output coefficients are obtained by dividing each element of the table by its corresponding column total (the output level). The input-output coefficients would then be (suppressing columns 3, 9 and 10, and rows 3 and 8, all the intermediate counts) as given in Table III.

TABLE III

	1 ind	2 n.ind	4 con	5 gov	6 exp	7 inv	8 sto
1 Industry	.133	.066	.244	.150	.722	.556	.556
2 Non-industry	.150	.150	.561	.173	.278	.222	− .112
4 Imports	.167	.100	.195	.075	–	.222	.556
5 Net Indirect taxes	.100	.100	–	–	–	–	–
6 Wages	.333	.400	–	.602	–	–	–
7 Gross profits	.117	.184	–	–	–	–	–
10 Total	1.000	1.000	1.000	1.000	1.000	1.000	1.000

The interpretation of the coefficients for final demand categories is the same as for production sectors. These figures can be used should one want to introduce the assumption of fixed proportionality.

The assumption that inventories should have a fixed 'input' structure is obviously nonsense. But for, say consumption, it may not be too far from the truth.

3.4. THE MATRIX FORMULAE

The input-output production model is specified by the following block-equations:

$$\mathbf{t} = A\mathbf{t} + \mathbf{f} \qquad (3.4.1)$$

Here $\mathbf{t}$ is the n by 1 vector of total production flows per sector of production. In Table II in Section 3.2, we have $n = 2$ and $\mathbf{t} = \begin{bmatrix} 300 \\ 300 \end{bmatrix}$.

A is the n by n matrix of inter-industry input coefficients. In the example we have

$$A = \begin{bmatrix} .133 & .066 \\ .150 & .150 \end{bmatrix}$$

$\mathbf{f}$ is a n by 1 vector of final output-flows (per sector of origin); in the example we have

$$\mathbf{f} = \begin{bmatrix} 240 \\ 210 \end{bmatrix}$$

For the demand for primary production factors, we will have a second block-equation

$$\mathbf{y} = C\mathbf{t} + \mathbf{h} \tag{3.4.2}$$

Here $\mathbf{y}$ is an m by 1 vector of required amounts of primary production factors or generated primary income flows in constant prices.

Counting all income categories, we would have $m=4$ and

$$\mathbf{y} = \begin{bmatrix} 140 \\ 60 \\ 300 \\ 90 \end{bmatrix}$$

$\mathbf{h}$ is a vector of direct final uses of production factors; in the example

$$\mathbf{h} = \begin{bmatrix} 60 \\ - \\ 80 \\ - \end{bmatrix}$$

The matrix C will be of order m by n in the example

$$C = \begin{bmatrix} .167 & .100 \\ .100 & .100 \\ .333 & .400 \\ .117 & .184 \end{bmatrix}$$

Should one also make the standard input-output assumption of constant proportionality for the final demand categories, we would have

$$\mathbf{f} = B\mathbf{g} \tag{3.4.3}$$

where $\mathbf{g}$ is a vector of final demand categories and

$$\mathbf{h} = D\mathbf{g} \tag{3.4.4}$$

The matrix of input-output coefficients is then partitioned in 4 blocks, as given in Table IV.

TABLE IV

	ind	n.ind	con	gov	exp	inv	sto
Industry	.133	.066	.244	.150	.722	.556	.556
	A		*B*				
Non-industry	.150	.150	.561	.173	.278	.222	− .122
Imports	.167	.100	.195	.075	–	.222	.556
Indirect taxes	.100	.100	–	–	–	–	–
	C		*D*				
Wages	.333	.400	–	.602	–	–	–
Profits	.117	.184	–	–	–	–	–

By (3.4.1) we will have:

$$\mathbf{t} = [I - A]^{-1}\mathbf{f} \tag{3.4.5}$$

The 'input-output inverse' $[I-A]^{-1}$ has a quite typical structure.[1] All its elements are positive or at least non-negative.

The matrix is rather dominated by its diagonal elements: all the diagonal elements are one or in excess of one. In (3.3.ex.3) we have, for

$$A = \begin{bmatrix} .133 & .066 \\ .150 & .150 \end{bmatrix}$$

$$[I - A]^{-1} = \begin{bmatrix} 1.169 & .091 \\ .206 & 1.192 \end{bmatrix}$$

By (3.4.2) and (3.4.5), we will have:

$$\mathbf{y} = C[I - A]^{-1}\mathbf{f} + \mathbf{h} \tag{3.4.6}$$

If we do make the restrictive input-output assumptions about final demand as well, we will have, by (3.4.3) and (3.4.5)

$$\mathbf{t} = [I - A]^{-1} B \, \mathbf{g} \tag{3.4.7}$$

and by (3.4.3), (3.4.4) and (3.4.5)

$$\mathbf{y} = [C (I - A)^{-1} B + D] \, \mathbf{g} \tag{3.4.8}$$

3.5. CUMULATIVE INPUT-OUTPUT COEFFICIENTS

The Tables III and IV of input-output coefficients (pp. 40 and 42) give the composite matrix

$$\begin{bmatrix} A & B \\ C & D \end{bmatrix}$$

Now consider the composite matrix

$$\left[\begin{array}{c|c} (I - A)^{-1} & (I - A)^{-1} B \\ \hline C (I - A)^{-1} & C (I - A)^{-1} B + D \end{array} \right]$$

This composite matrix can be written as given in Table V. This is known

TABLE V

	ind	n.i.	con	gov	exp	inv	sto
Industry	1.17	.09	.34	.19	.87	.67	− .64
Non-industry	.21	1.19	.72	.24	.48	.38	− .02
Imports	.22	.14	.32	.13	.19	.37	.66
Indirect taxes	.14	.13	.11	.04	.14	.11	.06
Wages	.47	.51	.40	.76	.48	.37	.21
Profits	.18	.23	.17	.07	.19	.15	.07

as a tableau of cumulative input-output coefficients.

The interpretation is as follows:

The first block-column gives the changes in production levels and factor-requirements, as are complementary with a change in the final output vector **f**.

Taking the industry-column, the tableau tells us that one additional unit of final demand for industrial products will require the system to produce 1.17 units more total output of industry; 0.21 more non-industrial products; use 0.22 more imports; yield 0.14 more indirect tax; require 0.47 more labour and give rise to an additional profit of 0.18.

The required imports, indirect taxes, labour, etc. are not just the amount going into industry itself.

They include the increased requirements of the non-industrial sector, due to the higher use of non-industrial products by the industrial sector. They also include the effects of the circumstance that the increment in industrial production is not just the one unit final output, but in fact 1.17 units. Industry must not only produce the one unit of final output, but also more semi-finished products to sustain the higher level of inputs into the other sector and into industry itself. Hence we give the name cumulative input-output coefficients, because of this cumulation of demand.

The interpretation of the second block-column is rather similar. For one unit of additional consumption, one initially requires 0.244 industry, 0.561 non-industry and 0.195 direct imports, and no other direct use of production factors. But the indirect effects include not just 0.244 units of industrial products, but $1,17 \times 0,244 + 0,09 \times ,561$ units of industrial products. And they include use of the production factor labour, due to the increased level of production to the amount of 0.40 units.

As is the case with most econometric models, we do not really pretend we can solve production and factor requirements for any final output vector, at any arbitrary level, but rather the emphasis is on variations over a limited range.

3.6. ALLOCATION UNDER CAPACITY LIMITS[2]

Consider the input-output Table VI, as printed on the next page. We will assume that this table refers to a historical period.

Legenda: t_1 = output of sector 1; t_2 = output of sector 2; i_1 = investment in sector 1; i_2 = investment in sector 2; c = all other final demand; and l = labour, measured in value in constant prices.

For the next period, the production capacities of sectors 1 and 2 are estimated at 210 and 310 respectively (i.e. somewhat larger than actually operated in the first period)

$$t_1 \leqslant 210; \quad t_2 \leqslant 310.$$

TABLE VI

		1 producing sectors t_1	2 t_2	3 $\overset{2}{\underset{1}{\Sigma}}$	4 final demand categories i_1	5 i_2	6 c	7 $\overset{6}{\underset{4}{\Sigma}}$	8 Total output
1 producing	t_1	20	60	80	25	35	60	120	200
2 sectors	t_2	40	90	130	50	40	80	170	300
3	$\overset{2}{\underset{1}{\Sigma}}$	60	150	210	75	75	140	290	500
4 labour	l	80	90	170					170
5 other value added		60	60	120					120
6	$\overset{5}{\underset{4}{\Sigma}}$	140	150	290					290
7 Total output		200	300	500				290	

The requirements can be written in the form of a system of inequalities. If we exclude disposal of final output we will have by (3.4.1) and (3.4.3)

$$\tfrac{9}{10} t_1 - \tfrac{1}{5} t_2 = \tfrac{1}{3} i_1 + \tfrac{7}{15} i_2 + \tfrac{3}{7} c \qquad (3.6.\text{ex}.1)$$

$$-\tfrac{1}{5} t_1 + \tfrac{7}{10} t_2 = \tfrac{2}{3} i_1 + \tfrac{8}{15} i_2 + \tfrac{4}{7} c \qquad (3.6.\text{ex}.2)$$

The additional requirements will be

$$t_1 \leqslant 210 \qquad (3.6.\text{ex}.3)$$

$$t_2 \leqslant 310 \qquad (3.6.\text{ex}.4)$$

and by (3.4.2)

$$\tfrac{2}{5} t_1 + \tfrac{3}{10} t_2 \leqslant 170 \qquad (3.6.\text{ex}.5)$$

It will be helpful to represent the set of feasible solutions in a two-dimensional graph.

Restrictions (3.6.ex.3) until (3.6.ex.5) can be mapped in the t_1, t_2 coordinate plane, as such.

For the input-output restrictions themselves, this will require a linear transformation. These restrictions initially involve 5 variables and 2 restrictions. But a mapping in the t_1, t_2 coordinate plane becomes possible, because of the non-negativity of each final demand category and then of any final demand flow as well. By (3.6.ex.1) we must have

$$\tfrac{9}{10} t_1 \geqslant \tfrac{1}{5} t_2 \qquad\qquad\qquad (3.6.\text{ex}.6)$$

and by (3.6.ex.2)

$$\tfrac{7}{10} t_2 \geqslant \tfrac{1}{5} t_1 \qquad\qquad\qquad (3.6.\text{ex}.7)$$

Relations (3.6.ex.6) and (3.6.ex.7) are not restrictive enough. If (3.6.ex.6) is binding we have zero final output in the first sector. However, we cannot invest in sector 1, invest in sector 2 or consume, without having non-zero final output in *both* sectors.

A more restrictive restriction on the minimal level of t_1 (the maximal level of t_2), is obtained by means of elimination of i_2. The vector i_2 is chosen, because this is the most 'sector 1' intensive final demand vector. Subtract $\tfrac{8}{7}$ times (3.6.ex.1) from (3.6.ex.2), to obtain

$$- 1\tfrac{8}{35} t_1 + \tfrac{13}{14} t_2 = \tfrac{2}{7} i_1 + \tfrac{4}{49} c \qquad\qquad\qquad (3.6.\text{ex}.8)$$

from which we have, by the non-negativity of i_1 and c

$$\tfrac{13}{14} t_2 \geqslant 1\tfrac{8}{35} t_1 \qquad\qquad\qquad (3.6.\text{ex}.9)$$

(3.6.ex.9) will be binding if $i_1 = c = 0$: if all final output is concentrated on investment in sector 2. A more 'sector 1 origin' mix of the final output is not possible.

The other restriction is obtained by eliminating the most 'sector 2' intensive final demand vector, which is investment in sector 1.

Subtract $\tfrac{1}{2}$ times (3.6.ex.2) from (3.6.ex.1), to obtain:

$$t_1 - \tfrac{11}{20} t_2 = \tfrac{3}{15} i_2 + \tfrac{1}{7} c \qquad\qquad\qquad (3.6.\text{ex}.10)$$

from which it follows by the non-negativity of i_2 and c

$$t_1 \geqslant \tfrac{11}{20} t_2 \qquad\qquad\qquad (3.6.\text{ex}.11)$$

An equivalent way of obtaining the relations (3.6.ex.9) and (3.6.ex.11) is by graphical methods.

To this end, one computes the cumulative demand for a certain amount of the two 'extreme' final demand categories.

46

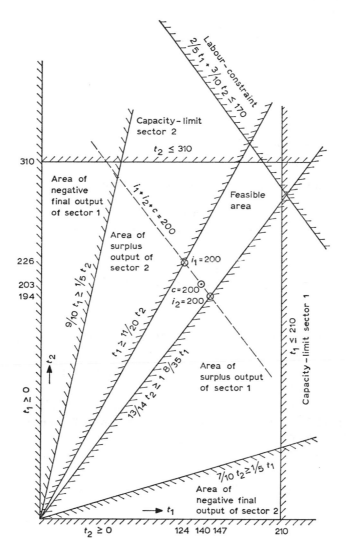

Fig. 1.

The required output-levels of the two sectors, for producing (200 units of) each of the three final demand categories only, are now obtained by (3.4.7) with

$$A = \begin{bmatrix} \frac{1}{10} & \frac{1}{5} \\ \frac{1}{5} & \frac{3}{10} \end{bmatrix}$$

and

$$B = \begin{bmatrix} \frac{1}{3} & \frac{7}{15} & \frac{3}{7} \\ \frac{2}{3} & \frac{8}{15} & \frac{4}{7} \end{bmatrix}$$

One obtains:

$$200 \times \begin{bmatrix} 1.186 & .338 \\ .338 & 1.524 \end{bmatrix} \begin{bmatrix} .333 & .467 & .428 \\ .667 & .533 & .572 \end{bmatrix} = \begin{bmatrix} 124 & 147 & 140 \\ 226 & 194 & 203 \end{bmatrix}$$

Or, presenting the matrix as Table VII, we obtain

TABLE VII

	i_1	i_2	c
t_1	124	147	140
t_2	226	194	203

The coordinates of $i_1 = 200$; $i_2 = 200$ and $c = 200$ are now plotted in the t_1, t_2 coordinate plane.

The feasible area is then limited by the lines between the two extreme points, $i_1 = 200$, $i_2 = 200$ and the origin.

The points $i_1 = 200$; $i_2 = 200$ and $c = 200$, are on a single straight line; the line of 200 units of final demand. The existence of this line is systematic: the rank of the system is only 2.

The slope of this line is nearly parallel to the labour-constraint. This is due to the fact that the cumulative demand for one unit of the output is almost the same for both sectors, namely 0.576 and 0.593.

The line of 200 units final output is then nearly the line of 117 units of labour.

3.7. ARTIFICIAL SECTORS

One may treat an accounting variable as a production level, even if there is no production in the physical-technical sense.

Possible reasons for doing so are: (a) simplification of mathematical formulae; and (b) extension and clarification of the accounting framework. Under (a) we note the possibility to arrange the tableau in such a way that primary production factors do not go directly into final demand. This can be done principally in two ways.

One way is simply to redefine the production factor as a produced good. The row is then taken out of the second block-row of the tableau and brought into the first (upper) block-row.

We will then of course have to define a corresponding input vector. The corresponding column will then have only one non-zero element, containing the total amount of the flow, once more recorded as a factor requirement.

Corresponding to Table II in Section 3.2 we might have Table VIII.

TABLE VIII

	1 ind	2 n.i.	3 imp. goods	4 con	5 gov	6 exp	7 inv	8 sto	9 Total
1 Industry	40	20	–	50	20	130	50	−10	300
2 Non-industry	45	45	–	115	23	50	20	2	300
3 Imported goods	50	30	–	40	10	–	20	−10	140
4 Imports	–	–	140	–	–	–	–	–	140
5 Indirect tax	30	30	–	–	–	–	–	–	60
6 Wages	100	120	–	–	80	–	–	–	300
7 Gross profit	35	55	–	–	–	–	–	–	90
8 Total	300	300	140	205	133	180	90	−18	

The same method could of course have been used for labour as well. In that case the bottom right-hand block would have been completely empty, but the number of sectors again are more.

The other way of emptying the matrix D is by treating final output flows as 'goods' by themselves. The level of a final demand category is defined as an output-level.

The same illustrative table might also be written as given in Table IX. In this case there is no final use of labour.

One could of course only account the public use of labour as 'produc-

TABLE IX

	ind	n.i.	gov	con	gov	exp	inv	sto	Total
Industry	40	20	20	50	–	130	50	– 10	300
Non-industry	45	45	23	115	–	50	20	22	300
Government	–	–	–	–	133	–	–	–	133
Imports	50	30	10	40	–	–	20	– 10	140
Indirect taxes	30	30	–	–	–	–	–	–	60
Wages	100	120	80	–	–	–	–	–	300
Gross profits	35	55	–	–	–	–	–	–	90
Total	300	300	133	205	133	180	90	– 18	

tion of civil service labour' and account the rest of public consumption directly as final demand. This is done by the British 1963 input-output table ([9], Table 19).

Artificial sectors can also be used, in order to make the accounting framework more realistic in detail. Consider the following example as given in Table X. This is a part of a supposed (fictitious) input-output table.

The *cost* of car production is 1,050 units in value. Of these 1,050 units at manufacturer's cost-price, 500 units are sold in the inland market,

TABLE X

	Some of the Producing Sectors			Final Demand Categories			
	Car production	Domestic car sales	Export car sales	Consumption	Export	Other	Total
Car production	–	500	500	–	–	50	1,050
Domestic car sales	–	–	–	750	–	250	1,000
Export car sales	–	–	–	–	700	–	700
Trade margins	–	100	–				
Other costs	1,050	–	–				
Indirect taxes	–	300	–				
Profits	–	100	200				
Total	1,050	1,000	700				

TABLE XI

	Imported goods	Consumer goods	Investment goods	Export goods	Consumption	Inv. (enterprises)	Gov. ivt.	Gov. salaries	Export	Stock acc.	Σ
Imported goods		2,532	2,843	2,500						,250	8,125
Consumer goods					10,000	6,000	2,000			,125	10,125
Investment goods										,125	8,125
Export goods									5,000		5,000
Imports	7,312										7,312
Indirect taxes	,813	,506									1,319
Labour		4,056	2,844	1,000				1,000			8,900
Gross profit		3,031	2,438	1,500							6,969
Σ	8,125	10,125	8,125	5,000	10,000	6,000	2,000	1,000	5,000	,500	

51

carrying purchase tax[3]; 500 units are exported, and a remainder 50 units are stockpiled by the manufacturers (disposed otherwise).

The 500 units inland sales, measured at manufacturer's cost-price, become 1,000 units when measured at showroom-price. The difference consists of: 100 units dealer's margin, 300 units purchase tax and 100 units manufacturer's profit. Dealer's profit is part of the trade margin.

On the other hand, the 500 units manufacturer's cost sold for export, become 700 units of export. The difference is 200 units of manufacturer's profit. Export is direct by the manufacturer and no purchase tax or dealers margin is incurred.

It is also possible to have *only* artificial sectors. In that case one has substantially a macro-economic account. The differential cost structure of the different final demand categories is accounted as if 'consumption', 'investment' etc. were a homogenous good, produced by a production sector. Such an account was in fact drawn up as a framework for having a consistent set of initial conditions for the short-term forecasting model discussed in Chapter II. See Table XI. One must assume the labour costs of the different final demand categories to be already cumulative input-output coefficients of the corresponding final demand vectors, based on the analysis of a real inter-industry table. The same holds for the use of 'imported goods'.

The data are fictitious. The fractional numbers arise because a table of input-output coefficients was written first, together with the totals of final demand categories. Corresponding 'total output' levels and factor requirements were then solved by means of (3.4.7) and (3.4.8).

3.8. THE INPUT-OUTPUT COSTING MODEL

Until now we have always treated value numbers as quantities and by doing so we have done two things:

(a) We have measured the amounts in such units so that the market prices in the period of recording itself are automatically equal to one.

(b) We have assumed these prices to stay constant. At least, this should be assumed if technical relationships of a strict complementary nature are to result in constant input-output coefficients in value.

But of course prices do change over time. We will assume that each good has the same price at all destinations. In some cases, where this is obviously untrue for the 'real' good, it can be made true by treating the same good at a different destination as a different good. (Compare the separate treatment of exported and domestically sold cars in the previous section.)

With that proviso, the one-good one-price assumption is fairly realistic. The device of 'splitting' a good should of course be used sparingly; otherwise the number of 'sectors' would approach the number of accounting entries in the original table.

Corresponding to (3.3.1) we will have, for a produced flow, which is an input:

$$p_i x_{ij} = p_i a_{ij} t_j \quad (i = 1, 2 \ldots n; j = 1, 2 \ldots n) \tag{3.8.1}$$

which is (3.3.1) *in value* (multiplied by the price).

The prices of production factors will be indicated as r_i. We will follow the notation of Section 3.4 and indicate input coefficients of production factors into production sectors as c_{ij}. Hence we have

$$r_i x_{ij} = r_i c_{ij} t_j \quad (i = n + 1 \ldots n + m - 2; j = 1, 2 \ldots n) \tag{3.8.2}$$

For the last two income categories, indirect taxes and profits, the concept of a price, if at all meaningful, will have to be defined. This is what we will do now, as follows:

Generally, proportional changes in either indirect taxes or profit-margins will be treated as price changes. If all rates of indirect taxes are increased by 10% of their former level (on a per amount basis) this is a 'price-rise' of 10%, and we would assume a new level of 1.10.

The same holds for profit margins. Changes in margins for individual sectors will be accounted separately, on the assumption that the general 'price' of profits and indirect taxes has not changed. By (3.8.1), (3.8.2), plus an additional term for changes in separate profit-margins, we will have:

$$\sum_{i=1}^{n} p_i x_{ij} + \sum_{i=n+1}^{n+m} r_i x_{ij}$$
$$= \sum_{i=1}^{n} p_i a_{ij} t_j + \sum_{i=n+1}^{n+m} r_i c_{ij} t_j + p_j^* t_j \quad (i = 1, 2 \ldots n) \tag{3.8.3}$$

Above p_j^* is the 'extra' price rise, due to changes in profit margin or rate of indirect tax, in that particular sector[4], and not to a general change in margins, and neither to changes in other prices.

As such (3.8.3) is an identity and trivial. This follows (3.8.1) which is (3.3.1) pre-multiplied with the price. But the left-hand side of (3.8.3) is *total output in value*.

$$p_j t_j = \sum_{i=1}^{n} p_i a_{ij} t_j + \sum_{i=n}^{n+m} r_i c_{ij} t_j + p_j^* t_j' \tag{3.8.4}$$

By (3.8.4) we will have, after deletion of the common factor t_j

$$p_j = \sum_{i=1}^{n} p_i a_{ij} + \sum_{i=n+1}^{n+m} r_i a_{ij} + p_j^* \quad (j = 1, 2 \ldots n) \tag{3.8.5}$$

This relation can now be expressed in matrix notation

$$\mathbf{p}' = \mathbf{p}'A + \mathbf{r}'C + \mathbf{p}^{*'} \tag{3.8.6}$$

The individual equations of the input-output costing model are read from the columns of the coefficients matrix, while the (primal) input-output production model follows the rows.

For example, if we limit ourselves to 'real' production factors the example in Section 3.3 would give rise to a price-cost relation for the first sector, as follows:

$$p_1 = 0.133p_1 + 0.150p_2 + 0.167r_1 + 0.333r_3 + p_1^*$$

Here r_1 stands for the price of imports and r_3 for the price of labour. We read along the *first* column of the coefficients matrix. The relation would assume an unchanged technology, as is generally assumed in input-output analysis.

Accordingly, the model would be realistic for ad-hoc price changes, but might be inadequate for a forecast over a longer period of time.

We now solve $\mathbf{p}'$ out of (3.8.6) and obtain:

$$\mathbf{p}' = \mathbf{r}'C\,[I - A]^{-1} + \mathbf{p}^{*'}\,[I - A]^{-1} \tag{3.8.7}$$

The index prices of final demand categories will be indicated as $\mathbf{d}'$ for deflators.

By the definition of an index number as a weighted average we will have

$$\mathbf{d}' = \mathbf{p}'B + \mathbf{r}'D \tag{3.8.8}$$

Substitute for $\mathbf{p}'$ out of (3.8.7) into (3.8.8) and obtain:

$$\mathbf{d}' = \mathbf{r}'\,[C\,(I - A)^{-1}\,B + D] + \mathbf{p}^{*'}\,(I - A)^{-1}\,B \tag{3.8.9}$$

By (3.8.7) and (3.8.9), the input-output costing model makes use of the complete tableau of cumulative input-output coefficients. In this connection it is worthwhile to recall Chapter II, Section 2.10. Here we stated: "The expressions within the brackets are based on accounting data (input-output analysis)." In fact these coefficients were transposed columns of $C(I-A)^{-1}B+D$ as obtained on the basis of Table XI, p. 51.

3.9. UNITS OF MEASUREMENT

Suppose we wanted to express a 1968 input-output table in prices of 1958. Consider an example as follows:

TABLE XII
1968 in 1968 prices

	ind	n.i.	con	gov	exp	inv	sto	Total
Industry	40	20	50	20	130	50	−10	300
Non-industry	45	45	115	23	50	20	2	300
Imports	50	30	40	10	–	20	−10	140
Labour	100	120	–	80	–	–	–	300
Other value added	65	85	–	–	–	–	–	150
Total	300	300	205	133	180	90	−18	

Let price-indices 1968 basis 1958 be known as follows:

industry   1.20   non-industry   1.50

imports   1.00   labour   2.00

We will then have 1968 in 1958 prices (Table XIII). Rows 'industry', 'non-industry' and 'labour' have been multiplied with the reciprocals of the price-indices.

The new 'total output' totals per row were copied as column totals at 250 for industry and 200 for non-industry. The row 'other value added' has been calculated afresh, by subtraction.

How does this operation influence the input-output coefficients?

The question is most easily answered for coefficients of inter-industry flows.

TABLE XIII

1968 in 1958 prices

	ind	n.i.	con	gov	exp	inv	sto	Total
Industry	33	17	42	17	107	42	− 8	250
Non-industry	30	30	78	15	33	13	1	200
Imports	50	30	40	10	–	20	− 10	140
Labour	50	60	–	40	–	–	–	150
Other value added	87	63						150
Total	250	200	160	82	140	75	− 17	

By definition, we have

$$x_{ij}^* = x_{ij}p_i \qquad (3.9.1)$$

Here, x_{ij} is the flow in the original table, which is the index-basis with the price of unity.

Then x_{ij}^* is the entry in the new table.

The transformation formulae would then describe the transformation of '1968 in 1958 prices' to '1968 in 1968 prices'. Or, alternatively, we should have listed the price-indices as 0.83, 0.67 and 0.50; for 1958 basis 1968.

For the total-level we will of course have

$$t_j^* = t_j p_j \qquad (3.9.2)$$

By (3.3.2) we will then have, for the new input-output coefficients

$$a_{ij}^* = x_{ij}^* t_j^{*-1} = x_{ij}p_i \left(t_j p_j\right)^{-1}$$
$$= x_{ij}t_j^{-1}p_i p_j^{-1} = p_i a_{ij}p_j^{-1} \quad (i = 1, 2 \dots n \,; j = 1, 2 \dots n)$$
$$(3.9.3)$$

The generalization of (3.9.3) to other input-output coefficients will be obvious.

(3.9.3) can be written as a matrix expression, by defining a diagonal matrix

$$P = \begin{bmatrix} p_1 & - & - \\ - & p_2 & - \\ - & - & p_n \end{bmatrix} \qquad (3.9.4)$$

of which the price indices are the diagonal elements.

We will then have (see Stone [51])

$$A^* = PAP^{-1} \qquad (3.9.5)$$

Above, we have treated the transformation of units as the introduction of new prices. This is the most obvious case of transformation of units in an input-output system, but the formulae are generally valid. All transformations of units will satisfy (3.9.1) and (3.9.2) whether or not the unit is interpreted as a price.

3.10. THE REQUIREMENTS OF PRODUCTIVENESS

Not all square and non-negative matrices can be input-output matrices A. Consider

$$A = \begin{bmatrix} 0.6 & 0.6 \\ 0.6 & 0.6 \end{bmatrix}$$

or

$$t_1 = 0.6t_1 + 0.6t_2 + f_1$$
$$t_2 = 0.6t_1 + 0.6t_2 + f_2$$

or equivalent

$$0.4t_1 - 0.6t_2 = f1$$
$$-0.6t_1 + 0.4t_2 = f2$$

This system solves as

$$t_1 = -2f_1 - 3f_1$$
$$t_2 = -3f_1 - 2f_2$$

As a result for *any* non-negative final output vector, the 'corresponding' total output vector would be negative. Also, let us require an arbitrary positive vector of margins for primary income flows per unit of output

$$\mathbf{z}' = \mathbf{r}'C \qquad (3.10.1)$$

We will then solve the system by the input-output costing model and obtain a negative vector of prices. The problem is that both production sectors use per unit of output, in total, more than one unit of inputs.

DEFINITION. A square and a non-negative matrix A is said to be productive if there exists an all-positive vector $\mathbf{f}$, and a corresponding non-

57

negative vector **t**, such that

$$\mathbf{t} = A\mathbf{t} + \mathbf{f} \qquad (3.4.1)$$

is satisfied. (Obviously such a vector **t** will also be all-positive.) The question arises which matrices A are productive.

THEOREM. If A is productive, the dominant root of A is less than one.

PROOF. First, we mention the relevant property of a non-negative square matrix. Any non-negative square matrix has a real and non-negative dominant root. The corresponding vector, both the row vector and the column vector can be selected non-negative non-zero. (See [15].)

As a borderline case, this includes the zero matrix, where the root is zero, and any vector is a characteristic vector. We will indicate this dominant root as α, the corresponding characteristic row vector as **w**′. Now consider a matrix A, and a pair of vectors **t** and **f** satisfying (3.4.1); **f** being all-positive and **t** non-negative.

Pre-multiply (3.4.1) with the row-vector **w**′, to obtain:

$$\mathbf{w}'\mathbf{t} = \mathbf{w}'A\mathbf{t} + \mathbf{w}'\mathbf{f} = \alpha\mathbf{w}'\mathbf{t} + \mathbf{w}'\mathbf{f} \qquad (3.10.2)$$

Since **w**′ is non-negative non-zero and **f** all-positive, we have

$$\mathbf{w}'\mathbf{f} > 0 \qquad (3.10.3)$$

and hence by (3.10.2) and (3.10.3)

$$(1 - \alpha)\,\mathbf{w}'\mathbf{t} > 0 \qquad (3.10.4)$$

Since **t** is all-positive and **w**′ non-negative non-zero, we have:

$$\mathbf{w}'\mathbf{t} > 0 \qquad (3.10.5)$$

Hence, by (3.10.4) and (3.10.5), we have:

$$\alpha < 1 \qquad (3.10.6)$$

The reverse of this theorem is also true. If the root is less than one, there will be a positive **t** for any positive **f**. In this connection we consider the expansion

$$[I - A]^{-1} = I + A + A^2 + A^3 + \cdots \qquad (3.10.7)$$

That the expansion (3.10.7) is indeed $[I-A]^{-1}$ follows by evaluating:

| the expansion | $I + A + A^2 + A^3 + A^4 + \cdots$ |
| *less* A times the expansion | $A + A^2 + A^3 + A^4 + A^5 + \cdots$ |

$(I-A)$ times the expansion $\quad I + \cdots$

If the root is less than one the higher powers of A will vanish (see [4]). This expansion gives rise to the typical properties of the input-output inverse, positive with a dominant diagonal. All powers of A are non-negative and as a result

$$\mathbf{t} = [I-A]^{-1} \; \mathbf{f} \text{ will be non-negative for all non-negative } \mathbf{f}.$$

Above, we discussed the productiveness of A in connection with the input-output production model, but obviously we must also have a positive solution to the input-output costing model, if and only if, A is productive. The relations of the input-output costing model are symmetric with those of the production model.

Substantially the same requirement in the above is also known under the name Hawkins-Simon conditions (Hawkins and Simon [25]).

3.11. THE GENERALIZED INPUT-OUTPUT MODEL

The following model is closely related to the input-output model, but of a more general specification; it admits for joint complementary outputs as well as for alternative process. We will discuss this model in terms of a particular industrial establishment, a factory. But this 'factory' may also be the whole national economy, where final outputs are evaluated as sales. In that case we obtain a planning model for a completely centralized economy. Hence we now discuss:

The machine-routing problem
Consider the position of a factory manager. He, the factory manager wishes to maximize the profit of the plant under his direction. This profit is defined as the proceeds of the outputs, minus the costs of the variable inputs, minus the fixed costs.

This problem admits for a solution by methods of linear programming. The purpose of this section is to formulate the problem in an orderly way, making use of matrix notation. It then emerges that the machine-routing problem is closely related to the Leontief input-output model.

Our notation for this problem will be as follows:

Let $\mathbf{x}$ be a column vector of levels of production processes, of order n;

Let $\mathbf{f}$ be a column vector of final output-flows, of order m_1;

Let $\mathbf{r}$ be a column vector of consumption-levels of raw materials and other variable inputs, or cost-items, of order m_2;

Let $\mathbf{c}$ be a column vector of fixed capacities, of order m_3.

We will then have the following system:

$$(A_1' - B)\,\mathbf{x} + \mathbf{f} \leqslant 0 \tag{3.11.1}$$

$$A_2'\,\mathbf{x} - \mathbf{r} \leqslant 0 \tag{3.11.2}$$

$$A_3'\,\mathbf{x} \leqslant \mathbf{c} \tag{3.11.3}$$

The system is defined by the capacity-vector $\mathbf{c}$, and two non-negative technology-matrices, viz:

$$A = \begin{bmatrix} A_1' \\ A_2' \\ A_3' \end{bmatrix}, \quad \text{of order } m_1 + m_2 + m_3 \text{ by } n, \text{ the matrix of input-coefficients}$$

and B, of order m_1 by n, the matrix of output-coefficients.

The model admits for joint complementary outputs[5] (more than one non-zero element in a column of B), and for alternative methods of producing the same good (more than one non-zero element in a row of B).

The columns of A and B correspond to production processes; the rows of A_1' and B to produced goods; the rows of A_2' to variable inputs; and the rows of A_3' (and the elements of $\mathbf{c}$) to fixed capacities.

To operate the jth process at a level x_j, will require an amount of $a_{ij}\,x_j$ of the ith good as input; and will produce an amount of $b_{ij}\,x_j$ of the ith good as output.

The objective function will be formulated in terms of $\mathbf{f}$ and $\mathbf{r}$. It is obviously wasteful to have slacks in the balance-equations of the first two block-rows. The shadow-prices of these restrictions will simply be the prices of the corresponding goods, as defined exogenously, except for goods whose external sale would result in a loss. Imputed prices of the fixed capacities are solved as shadow-prices of the binding restrictions in the third block-row.

Example
Consider a production process, indicated as p. One unit of p is assumed to produce 3 units of product p_1 and 4 units of product p_2, as complementary outputs. Three other production processes, indicated as q, r and s, are each assumed to produce only one single output-flow. These flows of goods are in this case identical with the operating level of the processes. Goods q, r and s are finished goods which are sold at prices 20, 25 and 10 respectively. Goods p_1 and p_2 are semi-finished goods, which have a zero sales price; but their production is required for the purpose of processing into q, r and s. Inputs of p_1 and p_2 into q, r and s are assumed as follows:

To produce 1 unit of q, requires 2 units of p_1, and zero p_2;
to produce 1 unit of r, requires 4 units of p_1, and 4 units p_2;
to produce 1 unit of s, requires zero p_1, and 1 unit p_2.

Processes p, q, r and s have variable operating costs of 1, 2, 0.5 and 0.4 per unit of operating level, respectively. The levels of p, q, r and s are limited by machine-capacities to 10, 20, 15 and 20, respectively. We will now formulate the problem in the form of a Simplex tableau; we will strictly follow the matrix notation of the theoretical part of this section.

The names of our variables will be as follows:
First, p, q, r and s for the levels of the four processes. Then $f(p_1)$, $f(p_2)$, $f(q)$, $f(r)$ and $f(s)$ for the final output levels of the 5 goods. And we will have v for the incurred variable cost.

The names of (the slacks of) our restrictions will be as follows: $b(p_1)$, $b(p_2)$, $b(q)$, $b(r)$ and $b(s)$ for the balance-restrictions of the five produced goods; $b(v)$ for the balance-restriction defining variable cost; and $bm(p)$, $bm(q)$, $bm(r)$ and $bm(s)$ for the restrictions on the machine-capacities.

The value of the objective function, which is to be maximized, will be indicated as τ.

We now obtain the Simplex tableau, Table XIV (next page).

We now readily identify the matrices:

$$A_1' = \begin{bmatrix} 0 & 2 & 4 & 0 \\ 0 & 0 & 4 & 1 \\ 0 & 0 & 0 & 0 \\ 0 & 0 & 0 & 0 \\ 0 & 0 & 0 & 0 \end{bmatrix}$$

TABLE XIV

Name	Value ≥	p	q	r	s	f(p₁)	f(p₂)	f(q)	f(r)	f(s)	v
$b(p_1)$	0	−3	2	4	1	1					
$b(p_2)$	0	−4		4	1		1				
$b(q)$	0		−1					1			
$b(r)$	0			−1					1		
$b(s)$	0				−1					1	
$b(v)$	0	1	2	.5	.4						−1
$bm(p)$	10	1									
$bm(q)$	20		1								
$bm(r)$	15			1							
$bm(s)$	20				1						
τ	0							−20	−25	−10	1

For three of the four columns, we have made the one-process, one-product assumption, as is standard in the Leontief input-output model. Accordingly, we have three unit columns in B. For one process, we have a more complicated structure. Should we make this assumption for all processes, B would become a unit matrix. As it is we now have:

$$B = \begin{bmatrix} 3 & 0 & 0 & 0 \\ 4 & 0 & 0 & 0 \\ 0 & 1 & 0 & 0 \\ 0 & 0 & 1 & 0 \\ 0 & 0 & 0 & 1 \end{bmatrix}$$

The large number of zeros in A'_1 is a direct result of the relatively simple structure of the example. Produced goods fall into two completely different classes: The goods p_1 and p_2 are semi-finished goods. They go as inputs into the processes q, r and s, but not back into p. The goods q, r and s are finished goods; they are not used as inputs at all.

$$A'_2 = \begin{bmatrix} 1 & 2 & .5 & .4 \end{bmatrix}$$

A'_3 is a unit matrix of order 4. This again reflects the specially simple structure of the example. There are no alternative uses of the machines. Accordingly, there is only one non-zero element in the corresponding rows of A'_3. Again, each process requires the use of only one type of machine. Hence there is only one non-zero element in the corresponding column of A_3'. We now readily recognize the anology between –

$$(A_1' - B)\, \mathbf{x} + \mathbf{f} \leqslant 0 \tag{3.11.1}$$

and

$$(A - I)\, \mathbf{t} + \mathbf{f} = 0$$

which is a rearranged version of (3.4.1), the standard input-output model. The same holds for primary production factors where (3.11.2) and (3.11.3) together will correspond to (3.4.2).

Now consider the programming problem:

$$\text{Maximize} \quad \tau(\mathbf{f})$$

subject to

$$(A_1' - B)\, \mathbf{x} + \mathbf{f} \leqslant 0 \tag{3.11.1}$$

$$A_3'\, \mathbf{x} \qquad \leqslant \mathbf{c} \tag{3.11.3}$$

We now interpret $\mathbf{f}$ as a vector of macro-economic final output-flows and $\mathbf{x}$ as the vector of all processes in a whole national economy. This then is an overall national planning model.

One must of course in some way deal with foreign trade. One obvious way is by assuming that imports are produced by exporting, and there are m_1 alternative processes for producing imports. Each 'import producing process' is the export of a particular good.

The assumption of infinite elasticity of foreign markets, up to a certain point, which is an export limit, may result in unrealistic outcomes of this model however. (See also Chapter VIII, Section 8.2.)

3.12. HISTORY OF INPUT-OUTPUT ANALYSIS

The idea of constant proportionality itself goes back as early as 1758. As such it is due to a Frenchman, Dr. F. Questnay ([42], p. 23), a physician of King Louis XV. But input-output analysis in the modern sense is intimately linked with the statistical recording of input-output tables. As such it goes back to Leontief [35].

In the Leontief system, there is a correspondence between final output and primary input.

Both aggregated accounting flows are total output, less inter-industry sales. Specific for the original Leontief model is the extension of the concept of a sector to final output and primary input. It is apparent that Leontief was thinking primarily in terms of consumption as final output. For example, in a later publication [36], he devoted a separate section to the concept of households as an industry. But this concept of a household sector defines away a meaningful group of questions. What happens to different sectors of production if, by suitable fiscal measures, a unit of purchasing power is redirected from consumption to investment by enterprises? or from investment to public expenditure? The Leontief concept of the square input-output table is well noticeable in the literature on input-output analysis. For example, Mattessisch [39] works out an input-output table where four 'autonomous sectors' are made to balance (Foreign sector, Government, Investment and Households). There are of course suitable accounting devices by which this can be done. But for one thing this suppresses any information about actual lack of balance between imports and exports, etcetera.

Statistically recorded input-output tables, except those compiled by Leontief himself, have no direct link between individual final demand categories and primary factor incomes.

On the mathematical side, the concept of an 'open' Leontief model is to my knowledge discussed for the first time in any detail by H. M. Smith [47] and by Dorfman et al. ([17], pp. 239–245). (An 'open' Leontief model is a model with an exogenous final demand vector as discussed in the previous sections.)

Leontief himself, notwithstanding his square tables, has analysed problems which essentially involve the open model (Leontief and Hoffenberg [37]).

The treatment of the input-output model in this chapter follows the Dutch Central Bureau of Statistics [6].

NOTES TO CHAPTER III

[1] The dominant root of A is less than unity. See Heesterman [26].
[2] See also Chenery and Clark [12], p. 95.
[3] It is assumed here that purchase tax is charged uniformly on all domestic first registrations (new sales).
[4] One might wish to assume constant profit margins (zero increment in p^*) for some sectors, and exogenous prices (zero increment in p) for other sectors. See: Bjerkholt [3a].
[5] For the treatment of this problem in a square system see Stone [51], pp. 39–42.

CHAPTER IV

SOME BUILDING STONES OF SECTORIZED MODELS

4.1. THE EXTENDED INPUT-OUTPUT MODEL

The input-output model is not by itself a complete model. It can be completed by adding relations for the volumes of final demand categories and the prices of primary production factors including profits. Or some factor-prices and volumes of final demand flows might be specified exogenously.

The simplest case is the constant prices model. In that case all prices are exogenous, and stay fixed at their historic levels. The input-output costing model is then of course superfluous.

It may be desirable to redefine final demand categories. With a somewhat larger number of final demand vectors, the constant proportionality assumption for each vector may become more realistic.

Example
Consider the following input-output table, for a closed economy.

TABLE XV

	production of							
	$t_{(1)}$	$t_{(2)}$	c	$i_{(1)}$	$i_{(2)}$	gi	pa	Σ
Sector 1	10	20	70	25	15	10	–	150
Sector 2	10	–	100	10	30	20	5	175
Indirect tax	15	5	–	–	–	–	–	20
Labour	80	100	–	–	–	–	20	200
Profit	35	50	–	–	–	–	–	85
Σ	150	175	170	35	45	30	25	

Legenda: $t_{(1)}$ and $t_{(2)}$, (total output) levels of sectors 1 and 2; c, consumption by households; $i_{(1)}$ and $i_{(2)}$ investment in sectors 1 and 2; gi, government's investment; pa, public administration.

The corresponding set of input-output relations would be

TABLE XVI

t_1	t_2	l	pr	c	i_1	i_2	=	gi	pa
.93	−.11	–	–	−.41	−.71	−.33		.33	–
−.07	1.00	–	–	−.59	−.29	−.67		.67	.20
−.53	−.57	1.00	–	–	–	–		–	.80
−.23	−.29	–	1.00	–	–	–		–	–

Additional Legenda: Two variables associated with rows of the input-output table, l = labour, pr = profit.

The indirect-taxes row has been deleted since the level of indirect taxes will not occur as such in the model. Under the assumption of constant prices, we must of course exclude any change in the rates of indirect taxation.

Variables gi (government's investment) and pa (public administration), are exogenous.

There are then 7 dependent variables, and as yet only 4 relations. Wanted are 3 reaction equations for final demand vectors, consumption and the two investment levels.

Copying the relevant relations from the short-term forecasting model in Chapter II, Section 2.2, we would have:

First introduce spendable income-flows

$$sl' = 0.80l' + 0.40\,(lf' - l') - ltau'$$

$$sp' = 0.50p' \qquad\qquad - lpau'$$

In the absence of variable prices, the distinction between volume and value is of course superfluous.

We now have the consumption function

$$c' = 0.85sl' + 0.40sp'$$

The investment equation is written *twice*, generally with different and separately estimated coefficients.

Filling in some coefficients, we might for example have:

$$i_{(1)}' = 0.6p_{(1)}'_{-1} - 0.3l_{(1)}$$

and for the second sector

$$i_{(2)}' = 0.5p_{(2)}'_{-1} - 0.2l_{(2)}$$

We are now again using the notation of increments and levels and suppress the explicit time-variable; a lag is indicated by a negative index (see Chapter II).

The relations correspond to long-term capital-output ratio's of 2.0 and 2.5 on total output and adjustment percentages in any year of 30% and 20% for each sector. The disaggregated investment equation will not be very satisfactory; at least not for all sectors. There is of course scope for piecewise adjustment in individual sectors. Some possible adjustments would be: (a) Taking into account longer time-lags or a distributed lag for some sectors; (b) Considering financial factors, influencing the financing of investment; and (c) Using ad-hoc information based on surveys, interviewing of businessmen etcetera. A labour-demand equation is already given by the input-output model as such. One obvious step towards a more realistic model, at least for short-term purposes, is to relax the rigid input-output assumptions for the demand for labour. Instead, one would have a labour demand equation of the type discussed in Chapter II, Section 6.

4.2. AVERAGE AND MARGINAL INPUT COEFFICIENTS

This is one of the possible devices for adapting the over-restrictive assumptions of the input-output model.

The basic relation for a single flow is now specified as

$$x_{ij} = a_{ij}t_j + r_{ij} \qquad (4.2.1)$$

instead of

$$x_{ij} = a_{ij}t_j \qquad (3.3.1)$$

Unfortunately, the statistical basis for estimating (4.2.1) is rather shaky.

Once we apply regression analysis we have to assume that x_{ij} is not subject to the influences of any systematic factor, other than the level of total output in the sector of destination.

This, however, is clearly not the case. First of all, there is the change in technology. Unchanged technology is assumed by the standard input-output model as well. Here (3.3.1) can at least be maintained as a valid estimate of the system, as long as the technology is the same as at the moment of observation.

But (4.2.1) requires at least two observations. Here a change of technology *during* the sample period will bedevil the statistical estimate. The estimates of the marginal input-coefficients may even become negative.

The second point is the price structure. Tilanus and Rey [55] report that they find input-output coefficients in *value* to be more constant than in volume. This is well in line with what one would expect on theoretical grounds. When the relative price of a good rises, its volume-ratio used as input by other sectors will fall.

Of course, this only confirms that the strongly restrictive assumptions of the input-output model are not very realistic.

The position is more favourable with the inputs in at least one final demand vector viz. consumption.

Consumption-flows from different sectors of origin do change systematically with the total, but not proportionally. Some 'inferior' goods follow the general standard of living less than proportionally, like food. Some 'superior' goods do not just follow the general standard of living, but increase rather more than proportionally, like motor cars.

Elasticities of the outlay on consumer goods, relative to total consumption, are normally estimated (Amundson [2]) on a logarithmic scale.

There is no particular problem in approximating the relationship on a linear scale. We will assume all consumption flows refer to produced goods, if necessary including outputs of artificial sectors. The linear relationship will then be

$$\mathbf{c}_t = \mathbf{c}_m c_t + \mathbf{c}^* \tag{4.2.2}$$

Here $\mathbf{c}_t$ is the vector of consumption flows (at time t). $\mathbf{c}_m$ is the vector of marginal input-coefficients, c_t is the level of total consumption (at time t), and $\mathbf{c}^*$ is a vector of level constants. The elements of $\mathbf{c}_m$ will add up to unity; those of $\mathbf{c}^*$ to zero. The elements of $\mathbf{c}_m$ are the partial derivatives of any sector-flow relative to the total

$$c_{im} = \frac{\partial c_i}{\partial c} \tag{4.2.3}$$

68

where c_{im} is the ith element of $\mathbf{c}_m$, and $\partial c_i/\partial c$ the derivative of the ith flow relative to the total.

They are obtained from the definition of an elasticity

$$\varepsilon_i = \frac{\partial c_i}{\partial c} \frac{c}{c_i} \tag{4.2.4}$$

which is solved relative to $\partial c_i/\partial c$

$$\frac{\partial c_i}{\partial c} = c_{im} = \varepsilon_i \frac{c_i}{c} \tag{4.2.5}$$

the ratio between the average and the marginal input-coefficients is the elasticity.

By definition of partial differentials we have

$$dc = \sum_{i=1}^{n} \frac{\partial c_i}{\partial c} dc \tag{4.2.6}$$

Hence the partial derivatives fit the input-output convention

$$\sum_{i=1}^{n} c_{im} = 1 \tag{4.2.7}$$

The level constants are now obtained by requiring the current solution to fit the specified relationship.

By (4.2.2) we will have

$$\mathbf{c}^* = \mathbf{c}_t - \mathbf{c}_m c_t \tag{4.2.8}$$

Pre-multiply (4.2.8) with a summation vector of n unity-elements, to be denoted as $\mathbf{s}'$, to obtain:

$$\mathbf{s}'\mathbf{c}^* = \mathbf{s}'\mathbf{c}_t - \mathbf{s}'\mathbf{c}_m c_t \tag{4.2.9}$$

Since $\mathbf{s}'\,\mathbf{c}_t$ is the column-count of $\mathbf{c}_t$ which is total consumption, c_t, the right-hand side will vanish by (4.2.7). The level constants will add up to zero.

$$\mathbf{s}'\mathbf{c}^* = 0 \tag{4.2.10}$$

4.3. STONE'S LINEAR EXPENDITURE SYSTEM

The idea of substitution between inputs on a price basis is valid for inputs in production sectors, as well as for final demand.

For production processes and investment there is the obvious difficulty of separating autonomous changes in technology from price-induced substitutions.

The relation between volume, total outlay and price is best treated in *value*. Following Stone [50], we will have:

$$p_i c_i = c_i^{**} p_i^{\P} + c_{im}^{\blacksquare} (C - \mathbf{c}^{**\prime} \mathbf{p}) \quad (i = 1, 2 \dots n) \tag{4.3.1}$$

On the left-hand side of (4.3.1) we have the value of the ith consumption flow, expressed as the product of its amount, c_i and its price p_i. On the right-hand side we have first a term $c_i^{**} p_i$. This is a 'hard core' subsistence level of volume-consumption. This amount will be bought irrespective of the price and the available income. c_i^{**} is the volume of this flow, which is exogenous; it is multiplied with the price to obtain a value expression.

The remainder of total consumption in value is then equal to

$$SC = C - \mathbf{c}^{**\prime} \mathbf{p} \tag{4.3.2}$$

where SC stands for surplus consumption in value.

By (4.3.1) this surplus consumption is distributed proportionally over the sectors, according to the marginal input-coefficients c_{im}. The c_{im} will satisfy

$$\sum_{i=1}^{n} c_{im} = 1 \tag{4.2.7}$$

The relation is linear, only in strict value terms. When it is expressed in terms of volumes and prices, it becomes non-linear. The non-linear term $p_i c_i$ can of course be approximated by a linear function.

Above, we have followed Stone, and explained the level-constants c_i^{**} as the invariable part of the consumption pattern. It seems logical to compare them with the level-constants c_i^{*} in a system of average and marginal input-output coefficients, as discussed in Section 4.2, which satisfy

$$\sum_{i=1}^{n} c_i^{*} = 0 \tag{4.2.10}$$

The c_i^{**} are somewhat similar to the c_i^{*} but, unlike the c_i^{*}, they need not add up to zero.

At constant prices, (4.3.1) will reduce to a system of average and marginal coefficients. All the prices are unity and we will only consider the volume of consumption.

$$c_i = c_i^{**} + c_{im}(c - c^{**'} s_n) \tag{4.3.3}$$

Here s_n is a vector of n unity-elements, being the (constant) prices.
Denote

$$\mu = \sum c_i^{**} = c^{**'} s_n \tag{4.3.4}$$

and (4.3.3) will reduce to

$$c_i = c_i^{**} + c_{im}(c - \mu) \tag{4.3.5}$$

or in a block-equation

$$c = c^{**} + c_m(c - \mu) \tag{4.3.6}$$

Comparing (4.3.5) and (4.3.6) with (4.2.2), we see that the c_i^{**} are related to the c_i^* by

$$c^* = c^{**} - c_m \cdot \mu \tag{4.3.7}$$

Or expressing the Stone-type constant in the input-output constants:

$$c^{**} = c^* + c_m \mu \tag{4.3.8}$$

Economically, μ represents the relative sensitivity of the distribution of consumption over the sectors, to changes in the price structure, or rather the lack of such sensitivity, for the relation is inverse, as may be illustrated by analysing two cases of possible values of μ. If we have $\mu = \bar{c}_t$, the parameter μ being equal to the level of consumption at a particular time, we see by (4.3.8) and (4.2.2) that

$$c^{**} = c^* + c_m \bar{c}_t = c_m c_t + c^* = c_t \tag{4.3.9}$$

e.g. the vector c^{**} (the 'hard core') becomes equal to the (level of the) current consumption vector, and the 'Surplus Consumption' is zero.

Also, it is possible to satisfy the original relation (4.3.1), after an increase (decrease) of one price, with Surplus Consumption remaining zero. All the c_i will remain the same (equal to c_i^{**}) and the value of consumption will increase (decrease) due to the price-rise of the one c_i; this increment (reduction) in the value of total consumption would cancel the increase in the value of the one term $c_i^{**} p_i$.

On the other hand, at $\mu = 0$, we have a system of average and marginal input-output coefficients in value, and if one price changes, (4.3.1) could be satisfied by the same *values* for each flow. In that case, a change in one price, while income, and presumably the value of consumption remain unchanged, would affect only one volume, that of the corresponding good.

With an increase in one price, there would be no reduction in the consumption of other goods so as to maintain the volume of the consumption of the dearer good within the same budget limit; and neither would there be an increase in the consumption of other goods because people would abandon the expensive good altogether.

4.4. UNEQUAL LAGS

The same variable may have a somewhat differently specified explanatory relation for different sectors. In the general case this will obviously allow a wide spectrum of models, a discussion of which is outside the scope of this book.

One special case is worth mentioning: The sector-relations for the 'corresponding' variable may be different only in the time-indices of their lagged relationships. The most obvious case is the relation between investment and production capacity, where we have the technical factor of a gestation lag during which new capital equipment is installed, fitted, adjusted, etc. but not as yet in productive use.

The point is discussed in some detail by Chakravarty [10].

The approach is potentially useful. But I am sceptical as to its usefulness in actually estimated models, until models are more refined and more realistic in other respects.[1]

For a short-term model, it will become difficult to identify relationships, with distributed lags, due to variation of output within existing capacity. For a long-term model the whole point of a gestation lag is of a somewhat lesser importance in any case.

NOTE TO CHAPTER IV

[1] See also Sections 6.2 and 7.3 concerning the stability of accelerator models.

CHAPTER V

CAPITAL-OUTPUT RATIOS

5.1. THE HARROD-DOMAR MODEL

Investment is part of output, and at the same time a means to increase output. This dual relationship was systematically studied, for the first time by Harrod and Domar [23, 16, 24].

The Harrod-Domar model is a macro-economic model, and as such it can be considered as a one-sector input-output model. As a result, some essentially macro-economic results of the dynamic input-output model can be traced back to the Harrod-Domar model. The still relevant part of the Harrod-Domar model can now be summarized as follows:

Harrod and Domar make all the simple complementary assumptions, which later become associated with input-output analysis.

At a given state of technology, there is a fixed linear relation between production[1] and the capital stock.

$$k_t = \kappa p_t \tag{5.1.1}$$

Here k_t is the capital stock, p_t the production capacity, which is equal to actual output, and κ is the capital-output coefficient. The identity of output and capacity is the essential characteristic of a long-term model.

Capital stock and investment are linked by[2]

$$k_{t+1} = k_t + i_t \tag{5.1.2}$$

By (5.1.1) and (5.1.2) one would then have

$$i_t = \kappa (p_{t+1} - p_t) \tag{5.1.3}$$

The investment, as meant in (5.1.2) either is only *net* investment, or one denies the need for replacement. Obviously, the first assumption is the more realistic one. Replacement is then dealt with in the same way as inter-industry deliveries; it is assumed to be a fixed proportion of the *current* output. Or it is exogenous.

We may also assume complementarity between labour and output

$$l_t = \lambda p_t \tag{5.1.4}$$

The implied assumption of constant technology and hence constant productivity is not stated by Harrod and Domar. They even speak about the need for inventions as a new opportunity for investment but this is a somewhat contradictory element in their theory[3]. They argue that to maintain full employment[4], one must have a certain percentage of investment[5].

By (5.1.3) and (5.1.4) one will then have the same growth rate both for labour and output and investment is solved as

$$i_t = \frac{\kappa}{\lambda}(l_{t+1} - l_t) \tag{5.1.5}$$

The Harrod-Domar model, by (5.1.3) alone is also used as a model for economic growth. A certain growth percentage is then formulated as a *target*. The corresponding savings ratio is then solved from (5.1.3)

$$\frac{i_t}{p_t} = \kappa\left(\frac{p_{t+1}}{p_t} - 1\right) \tag{5.1.6}$$

Here $(p_{t+1})/p_t$ is the exogenously required growth rate and the corresponding investment ratio is found by multiplying by the capital output ratio.

The following observation is now valid both on the macro-level (the Harrod-Domar model) and on the disaggregated level (the dynamic input output model). The concept of an autonomous growth rate of the output, independent of that of the population, is valid only if:
either
(a) The initial situation is one of substantial underemployment
or
(b) The constant productivity assumption (5.1.4) is dropped.

5.2. THOSE AWFUL DATA

When a model cannot be estimated such as to obtain estimated coefficients satisfying the a priori expectations of sign and order of magnitude, the operational value of the model must be viewed with a considerable degree of scepticism. Unfortunately, this is more or less the case with the Harrod-Domar model, and by implication with the dynamic input-output model. Only after introducing strong restrictive assumptions, can we obtain sensible estimates for the coefficients.

Consider the following data

TABLE XVII

	Average annual % increase in real gross domestic product, at factor cost, 1960–65	Gross fixed investment as % of gross National Product in 1960
United Kingdom	3.0	16
Austria	4.0	24
Brazil	4.4	17
Turkey	4.6	15
Denmark	4.7	19
Belgium	4.8	19
Italy	4.8	22
W. Germany	4.9	24
France	5.1	19
Canada	5.4	23
Mexico	6.5	15

Source: *Statistical Yearbook of the United Nations* (1967), tables 183 and 180.

For those countries for which later investment figures are available, the picture is not significantly different. (The investment does not vary all that much over time.) A glance at the figures is sufficient to draw the two essential conclusions: (a) A substantial part of the variation in investment is not at all related to variation in growth; and (b) Unless the constant is suppressed by specification, a substantial amount of investment is not at all explained by growth. In fact the regression slope is slightly negative,

$$\frac{i_t}{p_t} = 19.2 - 0.05 \frac{\Delta p}{p_t} \qquad (5.2.\text{ex.}1)$$

If one limits oneself to the developed countries only, a slightly positive slope is obtained (see Table XVIII).

TABLE XVIII

	Growth	Investment
United Kingdom	3.0	16
Austria	4.0	24
Denmark	4.7	19
Belgium	4.8	19
Italy	4.8	22
W. Germany	4.9	24
France	5.1	19
Canada	5.4	23

$$\frac{i_t}{p_t} = 18.8 + 0.1 \, \frac{\Delta p}{p_t} \qquad (5.2.ex.2)$$

However, the interpretation of the constant is that 18.8% of G.D.P. is needed as replacement. An additional investment has a fantastic return: the capital output ratio is only 0.1!

If we drop international comparison, we would then resort to time-series analysis. But here we are faced with similar difficulties.

A not inconsiderable number of countries combine a high growth rate and relatively little investment in the fifties, with more investment and a slower growth rate in the sixties. Year-to-year estimation of (5.1.3) is unreliable because of bad fit, due to short-term variation of output within existing capacity. No data on capacity as such are available.

Capital output ratios are normally estimated by fixing the constant a priori. This is done either at zero or at a rate equal to the fraction in domestic product arising from *depreciation*. Neat figures in the order of about $2\frac{1}{2}$ to 3 then come out.

5.3. THE ROLE OF TECHNICAL INNOVATION

Technical change is an essential prerequisite for increase in productivity. At any given state of technology, there comes a point where all production factors are fully employed in the most productive way. Resource limits will then prevent a further increase in production. This was recognised by the classical economists. For instance, Ricardo ([43], p. 124) wrote: "The natural tendency of profits then is to fall; in the progress of society and wealth, the additional quantity of food required is obtained by the sacrifice of more and more labour. This tendency, this gravitation as it were of profits, is happily checked at repeated intervals by the improvements in machinery, ... as well as by discoveries in the science of agriculture...".

Our modern problem is slightly different, at least in industrial society. Ricardo was thinking in terms of the limited supply of land. Under modern industrial conditions, it is the supply of labour which is the major restriction. But if we read 'consumer goods per unit of labour' instead of 'food' and 'more and more capital' instead of 'more and more labour', Ricardo sounds quite modern.

Johansen [30] and Solow [48, 49], have introduced the idea of 'embodied' technical progress. Investment is the vehicle by which technical progress is brought into an economy. Inventions only lead to higher productivity after new production processes are activated, and this requires new machines. This line is developed by Sandee ([45], pp. 162–183), who defends a linear output-capital ratio, much like the older Harrod-Domar one. But Sandee explicitly states a production function with substitution between capital and labour.

A marginal product of labour is effective for two vintages. With new investment one assumes 'ex-ante' substitution. Entrepreneurs have a freedom of choice to opt for different combinations of capital and labour, by moving along an iso-output curve. This freedom is exercised at the moment they install new equipment. Once installed the production function of any vintage is complementary. The other concept of marginal product of labour is at the near-obsolete vintage. Here is a one-way choice of scrapping. This marginal product is the entire labour-productivity of the marginal vintage.

But there is a snag.

The Sandee approach would be strictly correct, only in a macroeconomic model for a closed economy. In fact, it is used by Sandee and others, for sectorised long-term models. The obvious model for analysing inter-industry interdependence is the input-output model. Unfortunately, the input-output model assumes unchanged technology; the Sandee approach to the capital-output ratio assumes technical change!

In practice the problem is solved by applying a substitution-type production function on value added per sector. The complementarity – at fixed technical coefficients – between output and material inputs is upheld;

the complementarity between output and the primary factor labour is denied.

A rather arbitrary asymmetry which is plainly 'cooked' for the purpose of having a sectorised long-term model at all.

We have here an inherent contradiction which is to all practical purposes insolvable in the foreseeable future. Theoretically there is a correct solution, one would explicitly specify the technology matrix of the new 'vintage'.

But this assumes knowledge of a complete mapping of all possible production processes. This is of course not to be had.

5.4. THE COMPUTATION OF CAPITAL-OUTPUT RATIOS

Several methods of computing the capital-output ratio are due to Kuznets [34]. One method, following the linguistic interpretation of the name, is only possible if capital stock data are available. The stock of a nation's domestic capital is divided by its domestic product. Where no complete or reliable capital stock figures are available, one resorts to first differences. Or rather, Kuznets uses annual percentage increments.

By (5.1.1) we will have

$$\frac{dk_t}{dt} = \kappa \frac{dp_t}{dt} \tag{5.4.1}$$

By (5.4.1) we will have, after division by p_t:

$$\frac{dk_t/dt}{p_t} = \kappa \frac{dp_t/dt}{p_t} \tag{5.4.2}$$

The crux of Kuznets' approach to the incremental capital-output ratio is now as follows.

The factor $(dp_t/dt)/p_t$ is the rate of growth as a percentage per annum. The left-hand side is the share of investment in production. Kuznets now computes average percentages for both growth rate and investment percentage, over a somewhat longer period of time.

Theoretically, the ratio between net domestic product and capital stock should be the same as the net incremental capital-output ratio. The snag, however, is the valuation of capital.

Capital-stock data do not take into account the appreciation of existing assets, as a result of inflationary price-rises. This is a statistical problem which can be overcome by suitable methods of deflation.

But a more serious conceptional problem arises as well. Time-series data do not reveal how much growth is due to investment, and how much due to technical change, either 'embodied' or 'disembodied'. Technical progress of the 'embodied' type gives rise to a re-evaluation of the existing capital stock, for obsolescence. Capital stock figures are built up from investment data corrected for depreciation. Choosing the correct figure for depreciation then conceals the old identification problem: how to separate different causes of economic growth.

For this reason, the average way of computing is not really superior to the marginal one. They are really one and the same thing. Theoretically the average and the marginal net ratios should come out the same.

Capital-output ratios can also be computed on a linear basis. To this purpose, an example is now worked out (Table XIX) for the United Kingdom gross domestic product.[6]

TABLE XIX

Gross domestic product (market prices)

in 1958 constant prices	
in 1965	29.602
in 1957	22.716
Increment in production	6.886

Gross domestic fixed capital formation, in 1958 constant prices, in 1957 until and including 1964: 33.826. Capital-output ratio 33.826:6.886=4.9.

5.5. IN DEFENCE OF THE GROSS RATIO

From the accounting point of view, the *net* ratio would be the correct one. This is the reason for subtracting depreciation from investment in the first place. But consider the concept of a 'vintage-type' production function. We will use the same U.K. figures as in the previous section (plus some additional figures for manpower). The average annual increment in production is

$$\sqrt[8]{29.602:22.716} - 1 = 3.4\%$$

At the 1958 level this corresponds to an estimated increase of the capacity trend of $22\,785 \times 0.034 = 775$.

The production of the new vintage is this £ 775 million *plus* the loss in production due to wear and tear of the physical capital stock: *less* the increment in output due to non-embodied technical progress.

We now follow Sandee[7] and assume that the two corrections are equal. In order to know capital's contribution to economic growth we must subtract the contribution of labour. The increase in manpower[8] is about on a trend-level of 0.5% or 120000 man-years per annum.

At a wage-rate of £ 558 per man-year, the contribution of the increment of labour is evaluated as £ 56 million. In other words, only a quite insignificant part of the increment in output is the result of the increment in manpower. Capital's share in the increment in output is evaluated as £ 775 million less £ 56 million, or £ 719 million. This is not to say that the contribution of labour to the *total* production of the new vintage is so insignificant. But the contribution of the labour which is re-allocated from the near obsolete vintage to new investment is not seen. The two marginal products are assumed to be equal.

But then we should think about investment not so much in terms of increasing capacity as such, as well as of *modernization*.

By this notion obsolescence is the normal cause of scrapping, not technical wear and tear. But then the whole concept of 'gross' and net investment loses much of its meaning. On the aggregate level, the two are interlinked. Obsolescence is caused by new investment.

NOTES TO CHAPTER V

[1] The use of the same letter for two different variables cannot well be avoided altogether, the number of letters in the alphabet being limited. Hence the letter p, now means production, and also means price in some other sections. It is hoped that confusion is avoided by classifying the material into separate sections.

[2] Harrod and Domar did not in fact use period analysis but used the symbol Δ for increment, without specifying the precise time pattern.

[3] For a more detailed analysis of the interaction between multiplier models and technical change, see Robinson [44], in particular the *note* 'Mr. Harrod's Dynamics' on p. 404.

[4] Once one admits *substitution* either by way of a static differentiable production function, or with a vintage-type production function, the whole problem of full employment will vanish. At *any* level of savings (investment) there can be full employment given the correct factor proportions.

[5] Their problem is partly due to the specifically Keynesian assumption that the increment in *consumption* is a fixed fraction of the increment in production. In fact, this fraction can be adjusted by incomes policy and fiscal and other transfer payments.

[6] Figures from the 1967 'blue book' (*National Income and Expenditure*) [9].

[7] This whole section can be seen as a further elaboration of Sandee's investment theory. Sandee [45], already mentioned in Section 5.3.

[8] Calculation based on pages 24 and 32 of *The National Plan*. The order of magnitude of the figures is such that the precise employment figures do not matter much in fact.

CHAPTER VI

THE DYNAMICS OF ECONOMIC GROWTH

6.1. THE DYNAMIC INPUT-OUTPUT MODEL

The dynamic feature arises, because one way of disposing of the output is by producing investment goods. The production of investment goods is related to the increase in production capacity. This is a common feature between the dynamic input-output model and the Harrod-Domar model. But the single capital-output ratio is broken down per sector.

The capital-output relationship will of course hold for each sector of production. We will now distinguish between investment by origin and by destination. For each sector of production, (5.1.3) still defines the amount of investment which is needed to increase the production capacity with one unit. Consider the input-output table (XX), on the next page.

Not all investment is related to an increase in production capacity. Investment in agriculture and construction is treated exogenously. It is probably not much however.

Investment in public buildings is exogenous as well. On the other hand, it might be realistic to treat public investment in road-building as investment in transport.

About the (endogenous) investment in industry and services we will assume a capital output ratio of 2 for industry and 3 for services. Corresponding to (5.1.3)[1] we will have

$$i_t(2) = 2\left(ca_{t+1}(2) - ca_t(2)\right) \qquad (6.1.\text{ex.}1)$$

for industry and

$$i_t(4) = 3\left(ca_{t+1}(4) - ca_t(4)\right) \qquad (6.1.\text{ex.}2)$$

for services.

The transformation of investment by destination into investment by origin is defined by the standard input-output assumptions of constant proportionality.

TABLE XX

	Sectors of production					Endogenous investment				Σ
	Agri-culture	Industry	Construc-tion	Services	Imported goods	Industry	Services	Exogen-ous invest-ment	Other invest-final demand	
Agriculture		20	5	10	–	–	–	–	65	100
Industry	10	–	10	20	–	25	10	5	120	200
Construction	–	–	–	–	–	50	50	50	–	150
Services	5	10	5	10	20	–	–	–	75	125
Imported goods	5	15	10	5	–	25	20	10	40	130
Imports					80					80
Labour costs	50	75	60	40						225
Net indirect taxes	–10	10	–	15	30					45
Other value added	40	70	60	25	–					195
Σ	100	200	150	125	130	100	80	65	300	

83

In this example we would have

$$\mathbf{i}^* = \begin{bmatrix} - & - & - & - & - \\ - & .250 & - & .125 & - \\ - & .500 & - & .625 & - \\ - & - & - & - & - \\ - & .250 & - & .250 & - \end{bmatrix} \mathbf{i}$$

where $\mathbf{i}^*$ is a 5×1 vector of levels of flows by origin, and $\mathbf{i}$ investment by destination. Together with the capital-output ratios of 2 and 3 we will have:

$$\mathbf{i}_t^* = \begin{bmatrix} - & - & - & - & - \\ - & .50 & - & .375 & - \\ - & 1.00 & - & 1.875 & - \\ - & - & - & - & - \\ - & .50 & - & .750 & - \end{bmatrix} (\mathbf{ca}_{t+1} - \mathbf{ca}_t)$$

In general we will have

$$\mathbf{i}_t^* = K(\mathbf{ca}_{t+1} - \mathbf{ca}_t) \tag{6.1.1}$$

Here, $\mathbf{i}^*$ is a vector of investment per sector of origin; ca_t is a vector of production-capacity levels, per sector of production.

The matrix K is the matrix of incremental capital-output ratios.

Typical of this matrix is that its rank is generally less than its order. Note that the columns do not add up to unity, but to the capital-output ratio of the corresponding sector of destination.

As far as the dynamic input-output model is at all contributory to an actual forecasting model, this will be a long-term model. One will then identify capacity with output. Conceptually, there is an inequality relationship

$$\mathbf{t}_t \leqslant \mathbf{ca}_t \tag{6.1.2}$$

Here $\mathbf{t}$ is the current vector of total output levels per sector of production; $\mathbf{ca}$ is the vector of production capacities; the index $_t$ indicates time.

In any current period $\mathbf{t}$ must satisfy the static input-output model.[2] In a dynamic context we will separate investment from other final demand. For the simplified case of a closed economy without government, one will have

$$\mathbf{t}_t = A\mathbf{t}_t + \mathbf{i}_t^* + \mathbf{c}_t \tag{6.1.3}$$

Here, i_t^* is investment per sector of origin.

The vector $\mathbf{c}_t$ is the consumption vector. In that case we assume a closed economy without foreign trade, and also without government's expenditure. Alternatively $\mathbf{c}_t$ is all other final demand. But it will only be realistic to express this as only one final demand category if it is *mainly* consumption. There is of course an exogenous part of demand and output, which is completely outside the model. For consumption, we assume fixed *marginal* proportions of expansion. From Section (4.2) we have:

$$\mathbf{c}_t = \mathbf{c}^* + \mathbf{c}_m \, c_t \qquad (6.1.4), \text{ which is } (4.2.2)$$

The alternative possibility would be to leave consumption free, subject to a set of side-conditions.

This leaves the planner too much freedom. One would assume that the pattern of consumption could be adapted to what is possible or optimal. This is not realistic. One can control the level of consumption by means of macro-economic instruments. But its composition is largely determined by the preferences of the population.

Substitute for $\mathbf{i}_t^*$ by (6.1.1) and for $\mathbf{c}_t$ by (4.2.2) into (6.1.3), to obtain

$$\mathbf{t}_t = A \, \mathbf{t}_t + \mathbf{c}_m \, c_t + K \, (\mathbf{ca}_{t+1} - \mathbf{ca}_t) + \mathbf{c}^* \qquad (6.1.5)$$

Note that current inputs are related to actual produced output, and investment to production capacity.

There will also be a static requirement corresponding to (3.4.2). We do not now consider the direct use of primary factors in final demand. We will now explicitly consider the possibility of an inequality relation, of underemployment of production factors

$$\mathbf{y}_t \geqslant C \, \mathbf{t}_t \qquad (6.1.6)$$

Here $\mathbf{y}_t$ is the available supply of production factors which need not be fully employed.

Above, we considered the simplified case of a closed economy without government. To introduce public expenditure and export into the model, does not in itself create a particular problem. One simply adds the relevant terms to (6.1.3) and (6.1.5).

We will denote a vector of export-flows, per sector of origin, as $\mathbf{e}_t$ and a vector of other (exogenous) expenditure (including, and in fact mainly, government) as $\mathbf{g}_t$.

One will then have

$$t_t = At_t + i_t^* + c_t + e_t + g_t \qquad (6.1.7)$$

instead of (6.1.3), and

$$t_t = A\,t_t + c_m\,c_t + K\left(ca_{t+1} - ca_t\right) + e_t + c^* + g_t \qquad (6.1.8)$$

instead of (6.1.5).

The vector g_t may not only include public use of output in the conventional sense (the cost of public administration and, for instance, armament), but also semi-public investment, such as housing, investment in nationalized enterprises, public utilities etc.

The essential criterion is that of *exogenous* expenditure.

Of course, exports can be treated as exogenous as well, or there may be export-equations.

6.2. THE ACCELERATOR MODEL

Pure accelerator-type relations are not sufficiently realistic to justify their extension to input-output or other large-scale models.

This section was written in order to drive home this point. The temptation is there, to dispense with a full-scale accounting framework and a realistic price mechanism, and to base the demand for investment goods solely on volume-factors. Otherwise a sectorized model would become very large indeed.

Firstly, we remind the reader of our analysis of Section 2.8, which we will repeat in short here.

We assume that the investment decision (by entrepreneurs) is taken at the beginning of the current period, which is the end of the previous period. Known to entrepreneurs and industry managers then is: the previous period's output, and by their own previous period's investment, the production capacity of the forthcoming period.

The difference between the two, plus a constant is the basis of their investment decision. They invest to the amount:

$$i_t = \alpha\kappa\left(p_{t-1} + \beta - ca_t\right) \qquad (6.2.1)$$

Here κ is a capital-output ratio. Should they choose $\alpha = 1$ the investment would be sufficient to make the next period's capacity equal to the last observed output-value, plus the constant β.

Production-capacity is defined by a Harrod-Domar type production function

$$ca_t = ca_{t-1} + \frac{1}{\kappa} i_{t-1} \tag{6.2.2}$$

By (6.2.1) we can express the unknown production capacity in terms of observed variables and unknown parameters

$$ca_t = p_{t-1} + \beta - \frac{1}{\alpha\kappa} i_t \tag{6.2.3}$$

Substitute for ca_t and ca_{t-1} by (6.2.3) into (6.2.2), to obtain:

$$p_{t-1} + \beta - \frac{1}{\alpha\kappa} i_t = p_{t-2} + \beta - \frac{1}{\alpha\kappa} i_{t-1} + \frac{1}{\kappa} i_{t-1}$$

or

$$p_{t-1} - \frac{1}{\alpha\kappa} i_t = p_{t-2} - \frac{1-\alpha}{\alpha\kappa} i_{t-1} \tag{6.2.4}$$

Solve for i_t out of (6.2.4)

$$i_t = \alpha\kappa \, (p_{t-1} - p_{t-2}) + (1 - \alpha) \, i_{t-1} \tag{6.2.5}$$

which is the flexible accelerator investment demand function. Now consider the simplified assumption of a Keynesian closed economy

$$p_t = c_t + i_t \tag{6.2.6}$$

(Closed economy without government)
and

$$c_t = (1 - \pi) \, p_t \tag{6.2.7}$$

(Constant propensity to consume; the propensity to consume being $1 - \pi$.)
By (6.2.6) and (6.2.7) we have

$$p_t = \frac{1}{\pi} i_t \tag{6.2.8}$$

Substitute for p_t by (6.2.8) into (6.2.5), and write in homogenous form:

$$i_t - \left(1 - \alpha + \frac{\alpha}{\pi}\kappa\right)i_{t-1} + \frac{\alpha\kappa}{\pi}i_{t-2} = 0 \tag{6.2.9}$$

The dynamic behaviour of this system gives rise to the characteristic equation

$$\lambda^2 - \left(1 - \alpha + \frac{\alpha}{\pi}\kappa\right)\lambda + \frac{\alpha\kappa}{\pi} = 0 \tag{6.2.10}$$

Now consider the following 'reasonable' parameter-estimates:

Capital-output ratio

$$\kappa = 3$$

Coefficient of adaptation

$$\alpha = \tfrac{1}{3}$$

Propensity to consume

$$1 - \pi = \tfrac{2}{3}$$

We would then have

$$\lambda^2 - 3\tfrac{2}{3}\lambda + 3 = 0$$

Which solves as

$$\lambda = \tfrac{1}{2}\left(3\tfrac{2}{3} \pm \sqrt{1\tfrac{4}{9}}\right)$$

This should be considered as describing a violently explosive behaviour. In particular, at a rate of expansion of more than 2 times per period, investment will be considerably in excess of total production.

A less outrageous result is obtained by dropping the multiplier assumption (6.2.7).

If consumption is exogenous, we have to consider the possibility of a cyclical movement generated by investment alone, without a consumption-expenditure multiplier.

Substitute for p_t by (6.2.6) into (6.2.5), to obtain

$$i_t = (1 - \alpha + \alpha\kappa)i_{t-1} - \alpha\kappa\, i_{t-2} + \alpha\kappa\,(c_{t-1} - c_{t-2}) \tag{6.2.11}$$

The endogenous (investment) part of the system now gives rise to a characteristic equation of

$$\lambda^2 - (1 - \alpha + \alpha\kappa)\,\lambda + \alpha\kappa = 0 \qquad (6.2.12)$$

Our assumption about the parameters will remain

$$\alpha = \frac{1}{\kappa} \qquad (6.2.13)$$

The characteristic equation then solves as

$$\lambda = 1 - \tfrac{1}{2}\alpha \pm i\,\sqrt{\alpha - \tfrac{1}{4}\alpha^2}$$

The absolute value of this root is always unity. For $\alpha > 1/\kappa$ the system will give rise to explosive cycles; for $\alpha < 1/\kappa$ there is a dampening cycle. The parameter-estimate $\alpha = 1/\kappa$ may be unrealistic. But even at $\alpha = \tfrac{1}{3}$, $\pi = \tfrac{1}{3}$ and $\kappa = 3$, we would have for the multiplier-accelerator model

$$\lambda^2 - 2{,}6\lambda + 1{,}8 = 0$$

which solves as

$$\lambda = 1{,}3 \pm i\,\sqrt{0.11}$$

which again is an absolute value in excess of one.

Realistic models should preferably take account of all relevant realistic phenomena such as: financial limits on investment; tax- and import leaks; reduction of consumption due to increased prices.

Unfortunately, this would already be a fairly difficult task at the macro-economic level. Its breakdown into a sectorized model is likely to result in a very large and complicated model.

6.3. THE QUASI-STATIC MODEL

We now consider the costs of economic growth, stripped of short-term problems of dynamic stability. Oscillations of a business-cycle nature are assumed away. On the other hand, one essential dynamic element cannot be assumed away. This is the fact that faster growth will require a higher level of investment.

From a policy point of view, we can assume that oscillatory behaviour can be controlled by suitable stabilization devices or policies. But the need to invest cannot be dodged, only its timing can be adjusted.

The essential element of any quasi-static model is therefore a restriction on the time-path of all accounting variables. These are mostly medium or long-term models, referring to a planning period of 5 to 10 years.

The timing assumption is then one of continuity *during* the planning period. The time-path of certain key variables is then specific, except for two parameters: the level at the outset, the base-year, and at the end in the target-year.

The subject of analysis is of course the trend of long-term development, and any possibility to adjust this trend by suitable policy measures. One complication should be mentioned at the outset: Actual initial conditions may be 'abnormal'.

The last year of historical observation may be characterized by a situation which is not according to the long-term trend. This gives rise to the concept of the 'normalized' base-year. The base-year is fitted to the trend of past development by means of simple extrapolation. For instance, Lecomber [38] uses adjusted 1968 levels. The problem may sometimes be eased by the scantiness of statistical data. In this case, the statistical record of the base-year itself is largely non-existent, and 'normal' figures have been written in its place.

The time-path assumption may be linear as in Sandee's Indian model [46], or logarithmic, as in Sandee's later Dutch growth forecast [45] and in the above-mentioned paper by Lecomber.

The particular specification of the supposed time-path is not completely a question of convenience. Obviously the linear one is the more easy to handle, but the exponential one may be more realistic. The difference between the two time-paths will only be worthwhile if there is a relatively large increment during the planning period.

Consider the following simplified long-term model, which refers to a closed economy. The model refers to a terminal period, indicated by a time-index f, and a base-year period, indicated by a time-index zero.

The model will read

$$p_f = c_f + i_f + g \qquad \text{(accounting balance)}$$

$$k_f = k_0 + \sum_{t=0}^{f-1} i_t \qquad \text{(definition of capital stock)}$$

$$i_t = i_0 + \frac{t}{f}(i_f - i_0) \qquad (t = 0, 1, 2 \dots$$

(continuity restriction requiring investment to follow a linear time-path)

$$p_f = \omega l_f + \varepsilon k_f \quad \text{(production function)}$$

Legenda: p = production, c = consumption, g = government (public expenditure on goods and services), k = capital stock.

Parameters. ω and ε = productivity coefficients of capital and labour.

The exogenous variables are public expenditure, consumption and employment. Consumption will become endogenous in a programming approach. The same may be said in a technical sense of employment, though in fact one would want a full employment target to be satisfied.

The model may now be broken down into a sectorized model. Apart from the continuity restriction on investment, it will then be the dynamic input-output model.

By (6.1.1) we will have

$$\sum_{t=0}^{f-1} \mathbf{i}_t^* = K\,(\mathbf{ca}_f - \mathbf{ca}_0) \tag{6.3.1}$$

The increment in production capacity during the planning period is achieved by means of, and related to, the total amount of investment in the whole period after correction for the gestation lag.[3]

Note that: (a) the period $t = 0$ itself is the 'base-year' and as such considered as belonging already to the (recent) past; and (b) the investment in the terminal period $t = f$ itself, does not contribute to any further increment in production capacity.

But a linear time path for investment is required for the whole period. As a result, if investment is to rise at all, it must be at its peak in the terminal period itself. The linearity assumption is expressed algebraically by

$$\mathbf{i}_t^* = \mathbf{i}_0^* + (t:f)\,(\mathbf{i}_f^* - \mathbf{i}_0^*) \quad (t = 0, 1, 2, \dots f) \tag{6.3.2}$$

We now evaluate (6.3.1) by the sum formula for the arithmetic series.

$$\sum_{t=0}^{f-1} \mathbf{i}_t^* = \tfrac{1}{2} f\,(\mathbf{i}_0^* + \mathbf{i}_{f-1}^*) \tag{6.3.3}$$

The last term on the right-hand side of (6.3.3) is evaluated by (6.3.2) as

$$\mathbf{i}_{f-1}^* = \frac{1}{f}\mathbf{i}_0^* + \frac{f-1}{f}\mathbf{i}_f^* \tag{6.3.4}$$

91

We now evaluate the left-hand side of (6.3.1), by (6.3.3) and (6.3.4).

$$\sum_{t=0}^{f-1} \mathbf{i}_t^* = \tfrac{1}{2}(f+1)\,\mathbf{i}_0^* + \tfrac{1}{2}(f-1)\,\mathbf{i}_f^* \tag{6.3.5}$$

By (6.3.1) and (6.3.5) we will then have

$$K\,(\mathbf{ca}_f - \mathbf{ca}_0) = \tfrac{1}{2}(f+1)\,\mathbf{i}_0^* + \tfrac{1}{2}(f-1)\,\mathbf{i}_f^* \tag{6.3.6}$$

The other essential element of the quasi-static approach is the assumed identity between output and capacity, at least for the periods $t=0$ and $t=f$. For the final year this corresponds to the obvious fact that one will *plan* output to be equal to capacity. As a result, one will then *assume*

$$K\,(\mathbf{t}_f - \mathbf{t}_0) = \tfrac{1}{2}(f+1)\,\mathbf{i}_0^* + \tfrac{1}{2}(f-1)\,\mathbf{i}_f^* \tag{6.3.7}$$

We are now in a position to express the terminal year vector of investment levels per sector of origin as follows:

$$\mathbf{i}_f^* = \frac{2}{f-1}\,K\,\mathbf{t}_f - \frac{2}{f-1}\,K\,\mathbf{t}_0 - \frac{f+1}{f-1}\,\mathbf{i}_0^* \tag{6.3.8}$$

By (6.3.8) and (6.1.7), we will then have

$$\mathbf{t}_f = \left[A + \frac{2}{f-1}\,K\right]\mathbf{t}_f + \mathbf{c}_f + \mathbf{e}_f + \mathbf{g}_f - \frac{2}{f-1}\,K\,\mathbf{t}_0 - \frac{f+1}{f-1}\,\mathbf{i}_0^* \tag{6.3.9}$$

The composite matrix

$$Q = A + \frac{2}{f-1}\,K \tag{6.3.10}$$

may be named the matrix of quasi-static input coefficients.

It is here assumed that Q does satisfy the requirement of productivity, hence, has a dominant latent root of less than 1. (See Section 3.10.) There is of course no inherent requirement that Q should have this property for all f. On the contrary, if the planning period is short, the dominant root of Q will be in excess of unity.

But a meaningful evaluation of a plan by means of a quasi-static model is possible only if Q is productive. This corresponds to the fact that (for a short planning period) more consumption, more public expenditure etc. are to be had, not so much by producing more, but rather by having less investment. The question of the relative productiveness of the different sectors will then become irrelevant.

This is seen most clearly with a somewhat simplified model, corresponding to (6.1.3). Grouping all final output except investment together as 'consumption' we will have by (6.3.8) and (6.3.10)

$$t_f = Q\,t_f + c_f - \frac{2}{f-1}\,K\,t_0 - \frac{f+1}{f-1}\,i_0^* \qquad (6.3.11)$$

Solve for t_f

$$t_f = [I - Q]^{-1}\,c_f - [I - Q]^{-1}\left(\frac{2}{f-1}\,K\,t_0 + \frac{f+1}{f-1}\,i_0^*\right)$$

$$(6.3.12)$$

If $[I-Q]^{-1}$ has the 'normal' input-output properties, more consumption (generally more final output, other than investment) automatically means more production. Under these conditions, (6.3.9) or (6.3.12) can help in comparing the relative costliness of sectors in terms of primary production factors. In the 'reverse' case, there may still be a solution to (6.3.12).

But now the analogy with the static input-output model is lost.

6.4. THE NATIONAL PLAN

Consider the following programming problem:

  Maximize c_f

subject to

$$t_f = Q\,t_f + c_m\,c_f + e_f +$$
$$+ c^* + g_f - \frac{2}{f-1}\,K\,t_0 - \frac{f+1}{f-1}\,i_0^* \qquad (6.4.1)$$

and

$$c_1'\,t_f = s_n'\,e_f + ci \qquad (6.4.2)$$

and

$$c_2'\,t_f \leqslant 1_f \qquad (6.4.3)$$

$$e_f \leqslant el_f \qquad (6.4.4)$$

$$s_n'\,i_f^* \leqslant \alpha\,c_2'\,t_f + \beta\,c_3'\,t_f \qquad (6.4.5)$$

Above (6.4.1) is the quasi-static balance of production by (6.3.9) and (6.3.10). The term for consumption c_t is replaced by its expression in a ma-

93

cro-level and marginal coefficients per sector by (4.2.2). The second line of the right-hand side of (6.4.1) gives the exogenous terms: the constants vector c^*, the government's expenditure g_f and the initial conditions contribution in (6.3.9).

The additional restrictions are:

(6.4.2) A balance of payments restriction. It is assumed that imports are listed as the first non-produced [4] good. Total imports, as solved by the input-output model, is required to equal total exports (the exports vector pre-multiplied with a summation vector s'_n) plus an exogenous constant, ci for capital import. The exogenous capital import may be positive, zero or negative, according to which balance of payments target is set.

(6.4.3) A labour balance. The demand for labour, as resulting from production cannot exceed its supply.

(6.4.4) A block of export limits, at the levels of el_f. For each sector there is a ceiling on what can be absorbed by foreign markets. This limit may be zero in the case of a non-tradeable good, for instance, construction or rail transport. For some sectors, a net import may also be represented as a negative export.

(6.4.5) The last restriction is one on the financing of investment. It is assumed that the second row [4] of C is the labour row and the third the profits row. The value of investment is restricted to being less than a linear function of wages and profits. The equation is in fact given here in a simplified form; it may have to be adjusted for changes in prices.

Two groups of application of this model can now be mentioned. On the one side we have development plans for underdeveloped economies. Indeed, our exposition of the quasi-static model closely follows Sandee's Indian model [46]. In this case the labour balance will normally be a superfluous restriction. The model was then run on the basis of the historically observed input-output coefficients and capital-output ratios. But the model can be applied to developed economies as well, be it with some qualifications.

The preparation of a National Plan is very much a two-way flow of information, between industry committees on the one side and the central planning agency on the other side.

With a binding labour balance in the initial situation, any substantial increment in final output must assume increases in productivity. Technical change is an essential part of the plan.

94

The relevant input-output coefficients and capital-output ratios are then not the ones historically recorded, but the ones to be obtained from industries' plans.

But the industry-plans are not formulated in a vacuum. The government, or the central planning organization on its behalf will give certain signals, notably:

(a) an expected price-structure, a price-forecast, including a wage-rate forecast. The impact of the price-structure on the choice of particular production processes falls outside the scope of this book.

But it seems reasonable to assume that at a given set of prices, the technology is invariant to output-levels and the input-output model is applicable.

(b) an expected level of gross domestic production, national income etcetera, and the output level of each sector (the column totals of the input-output table).

This initial central forecast can be thought of as being drawn up more or less 'out of the blue', that is by extrapolating past trends.[5]

But it would set an output-target for each sector.

Sector-committees would now be asked to state their industries requirements in terms of current inputs of other produced goods, imports, manpower, and investment in fixed assets, that would be needed in order to sustain the set target in terms of total output. They would also be asked to indicate how much they thought they could sell abroad, given a sufficient domestic supply-capacity. Most likely, the results of this first-round would not provide a ready-made National Plan.

Row-counts of the input-output table as resulting from industries' answers, would not match the set output targets and the macro-economic side-restrictions. But the planning organization would now know where future technical coefficients were likely to differ from the historical ones.

Now the model can be used to obtain a consistent plan.

One essential point of modification of the model should be mentioned here. The investment will be split in two components: modernization and expansion, as far as this is possible. The modernization investment is linked to the change in the static input-output coefficients. It is then exogenous; in the next model-run both input-output coefficients and modernization-investment are kept constant. Incremental capital output ratios are computed on the basis of the expansion part of the investment only. The modernization-investment is changed to the production-balance as an exogenous requirement, similar to replacement or public expenditure.

Example:

Consider the input-output Table XXI for a closed economy.

TABLE XXI

| | production of | | | | | | | |
	$t_{(1)}$	$t_{(2)}$	c	$i_{(1)}$	$i_{(2)}$	gi	pa	Σ
Sector 1	10	20	70	25	15	10	–	150
Sector 2	10	–	100	10	30	20	5	175
Indirect tax	15	5	–	–	–	–	–	20
Labour	80	100	–	–	–	–	20	200
Profit	35	50	–	–	–	–	–	85
Σ	150	175	170	35	45	30	25	

Legenda. $t_{(1)}$ and $t_{(2)}$ (total output) levels of sectors 1 and 2; c, consumption by households; $i_{(1)}$ and $i_{(2)}$ investment in sectors 1 and 2; $gi=$ government investment; $pa=$ public administration. This is the example of Section 4.1.

We now suppose this to be a historical table, describing a 'base-year' $t=0$. An initial central forecast is now made up for the year $t=f$. Final demand in constant prices, controlled by public policy instruments:

TABLE XXII

	c	gi	pa
Sector 1	90	11	
Sector 2	120	22	5
Labour			20
Σ	210	33	25

sectorwise production totals in constant prices

$$t_1 = 200 \qquad t_2 = 205$$

96

prices:

$$p_1 = 1.00 \text{ (unchanged)}; \quad p_2 = 1.05; \quad r_2 = 1.35 \text{ (35\%}$$
wage increase); indirect taxes unchanged.

As a result of industry's information, we now obtain Tables XXIII and XXIV.

TABLE XXIII

(In constant prices)

	t_1	t_2	c	i_1	i_2	gi	pa	Σ
Sector 1	14	22	90	30	20	11	–	187
Sector 2	12	–	120	10	30	22	5	199
Indirect tax	20	6	–	–	–	–	–	26
Labour	80	95	–	–	–	–	20	195
Profit	74	82	–	–	–	–	–	156
Σ	200	205	210	40	50	33	25	

TABLE XXIV

(In forecasted prices)

	t_1	t_2	c	i_1	i_2	gi	pa	Σ
Sector 1	14	22	90	30	20	11	–	187
Sector 2	13	–	126	11	32	23	5	210
Indirect tax	20	6	–	–	–	–	–	26
Labour	108	128	–	–	–	–	27	263
Profit	45	59	–	–	–	–	–	104
Σ	200	215	216	41	52	34	32	

There are a few rather striking features about Tables XXIII and XXIV. They certainly do not provide an acceptable plan. There is an actual contraction of employment and the sector-rows do not balance to the sector-column totals. (The column-totals correspond to the set targets.)

But they do contain some relevant information. We will for the moment limit ourselves to the application of the quasi-static input-output model.

A consistent and 'optimal' plan can be obtained in two directions.

Full employment of labour can be achieved by increasing the level of activity. This of course will result in even higher investment levels.

On the other hand, if we introduce a finance-capital restriction, it could well be that a full employment target would have to be abandoned, at least at this set of technical coefficients.

We will for the moment make the first assumption: we will maintain the full-employment target and not introduce a finance-capital restriction. The alternative would of course be a linear programming model.

We will assume that half of the investment going into sector 1 is for expansion, the remaining half for replacement and modernization; the corresponding percentage-distribution being assumed to be one third expansion and two thirds replacement and modernization for sector 2.

We now infer the following static input-output coefficients (in constant prices), as given in Table XXV.

TABLE XXV

	t_1	t_2	c	i_1	i_2
Sector 1	.07	.11	.43	.75	.40
Sector 2	.06	–	.57	.25	.60
Labour	.40	.46			

For exogenous expenditure, we have Table XXVI.

TABLE XXVI

	ei	gi	pa	Σ
Sector 1	28	11	–	39
Sector 2	25	22	5	52
Labour	–	–	20	20

Legenda. ei=enterprises' investment (replacement and modernization only); gi=governments' investment; and pa=public administration.

We will assume a full-employment target of 205. This leaves for employment in the two sectors: $205-20=185$.

We will then have the set of static requirements as given in Table XXVI.

TABLE XXVI

	t_1	t_2	c	i_1	i_2		
Sector 1	.93	−.11	−.43	−.75	−.40	=	39
Sector 2	−.06	1.00	−.57	−.25	−.60	=	52
Labour	−.40	−.46				=	−185

This table is comparable with Table XVI in Section 4.1 except for the different presentation of the labour-row and the deletion of the profits row.

But the data are not those of historical observation, but inferred from industries' answers to the question: Given such and such a marketing position, how would you react; what would you want to buy yourself?

Now consider the capital-output ratios.

Total expansion-investment in sector 1 will be half of the total investment in years $t=0$ until 4, or half of $\frac{1}{2}.5$ $(35+39)=$half of 185 or 93.

The increment in output is $200-150=50$; the capital output ratio is 1.85.

And for sector 2: one third of $\frac{1}{2}.5$ $(45+49)=235$ units of investment, of which 78 are for expansion. The increment in output is $(205-175)=30$; a capital-output ratio of 2.60.

The matrix K of (6.3.8) is now evaluated by multiplying the i_1 column with 1.85 and the i_2 column with 2.60.

146748

$$
K = \begin{array}{c} \text{sector 1} \\ \text{sector 2} \end{array} \begin{array}{cc} i_1 & i_2 \\ \begin{bmatrix} 1.39 & 1.04 \\ .46 & 1.56 \end{bmatrix} \end{array}
$$

We now write out (6.3.8) in extenso, with $2/(f-1)=\frac{1}{2}$.

$$
i_f^* = \begin{bmatrix} .69 & .52 \\ .23 & .78 \end{bmatrix} t_f - \begin{bmatrix} .69 & .52 \\ .23 & .78 \end{bmatrix} t_0 - \tfrac{6}{4} i_0^*. \tag{6.4.ex.1}
$$

The quasi-static interindustry-cost matrix Q is evaluated by (6.3.10)

$$
Q = \begin{bmatrix} .07 & .11 \\ .06 & - \end{bmatrix} + \tfrac{1}{2} \begin{bmatrix} 1.39 & 1.04 \\ .46 & 1.56 \end{bmatrix} = \begin{bmatrix} .76 & .63 \\ .29 & .78 \end{bmatrix} \tag{6.4.ex.2}
$$

The model is now written out in extenso in Table XXVII. For a number of reasons, the example is not well suited as an actual planning model. For one thing, the quasi-static matrix Q does not satisfy the Hawkins-Simon conditions.

We do in fact have the 'reverse' case. Because Q is not productive, more consumption is to be had by less investment and not by more production. One might think, however, that one could still solve the model. This is true as far as the algebra goes. But it overlooks one important point. The essential element of consistency of the plan is that it should create a set

TABLE XXVII

	$t_1(f)$	$t_2(f)$	c	$i^*_1(f)$	$i^*_2(f)$	$t_1(0)$	$t_2(0)$	$i^*_1(0)$	$i^*_2(0)$	=	
Sector 1	.93	−.11	−.43	−1.00	–	–	–	–	–	=	39
Sector 2	−.06	1.00	−.57	–	−1.00	–	–	–	–	=	52
Labour	−.40	−.46	–	–	–	–	–	–	–	=	−185
i^*_1	−.69	−.52	–	1.00	–	.69	.52	1.50	–	=	–
i^*_2	−.23	−.78	–	–	1.00	.23	.78	–	1.50	=	–
	–	–	–	–	1.00	–	–	–	–	=	150
initial	–	–	–	–	–	–	1.00	–	–	=	175
conditions	–	–	–	–	–	–	–	1.00	–	=	18
	–	–	–	–	–	–	–	–	1.00	=	15

of expectations, which will induce entrepreneurs to buy such quantities of current inputs and investment goods as will actually sustain those expectations.

But investment decisions are supposed to be based on the long-term expectation. The 'reverse' case can hardly qualify as long term in this respect.

The supposed optimality of the model-outcome should not be overemphasised, even if it is a true plan in the sense that expectations and the corresponding entrepreneurial reactions are consistent. The information as actually given by the sector-committees, would not give a full mapping of all technical possibilities, but only an indication of industry's most likely reaction to certain external conditions, as simulated by the first central forecast. One further step towards insuring feasibility of the plan would be to issue a new central forecast, and to verify that industry's reaction on the new central forecast confirms the model. If there would still be differences, the exercise could be repeated.

But more important, it is possible that a 'better' solution could be obtained by means of certain positive policies in order to influence the choice of technology. This would be particularly the case if the model would be limited by some of the macro-economic restrictions, others being amply fulfilled.

Should for instance, the labour balance be binding, but a restriction on finance-capital be amply fulfilled, there is a case for fiscal and other facilities favouring modernization, in order to increase labour productivity, even when this will cost more investment.

Should a finance-capital restriction be binding, and the labour-balance be amply fulfilled, the opposite will be the case.

NOTES TO CHAPTER VI

[1] Note that we now again use the symbol *ca* for production capacity, instead of *p* for production. This corresponds to the fact that we have dropped the assumption that output equals production capacity.

[2] See Chapter III, Sections 3.4 and 3.6. The exogenous constants of 210 and 310 in Sextion 3.6 will be replaced by the vector ca_t, which is now variable in a dynamic context.

[3] This implies a gestation lag of half a period (year). The length of the gestation lag is of course rather arbitrary. One has to put some figure.

[4] The letter C was chosen in analogy with Chapter III. The vectors c'_1, c'_2 and c'_3 are then rows of a matrix of factor-input coefficients. They should not be confused with consumption!

[5] In fact, the setting of higher initial targets will almost certainly stimulate innovation and imaginative planning by sectors. But this 'announcement effect' falls outside the scope of the technological-econometric approach.

CHAPTER VII

DYNAMIC ADJUSTMENT MODELS AND THEIR CONVERGENCE*

7.1. THE DICHOTOMY

There are two groups of models. The one type of model is designed to forecast the immediate future. The other type is concerned with the analysis of structural change and economic growth. The dichotomy goes back to the underlying economic theory. There are not only two groups of models, but there were two groups of economic theories well before there were formal models.

One group of models and the corresponding group of theories is essentially dynamic. The other group of models and theories pre-supposes that cyclical and other fluctuations will always converge to some equilibrium conditions, and wants to analyse the equilibrium itself.

The idea may be illustrated by means of a mechanical example: We observe a child on a swing. One now wants to forecast the position of the swing after fifty seconds. This (short term) model will be in terms of the swing's initial position and speed. It will calculate the length and frequency of the swinging movement. It may perhaps consider exogenous information, such as the fact that a parent is giving the child a push at the beginning of three successive sways of the swing.

Now consider the long-term model. If we want to forecast the position of the swing after five minutes, we will realize that it is impossible to forecast the precise rhythm of the swing with sufficient accuracy over such a long period of time. The long-term model will assume that the swing is in neutral position, and only consider the position of the poles. Actual applied models are not really static models in this sense. There is always some element of dynamics, notably the concept of the capital-output ratio. The rate of growth is related to the level of investment, but one assumes a constant rate of growth over a longer period of time. The focus of attention is on the relation between different rates of growth with changes in the structure of the economy, the relative levels of different activities in the economy.

7.2. THE CAUSAL CHAIN

Consider the following line of thought: Our object is the causal relationship between past, present and future. Algebraically, a causal relationship is of course at the same time a functional one. If phenomenon A is caused by phenomenon B, then a linear model will say that variable A is a linear function of variable B, and that is algebraically equivalent with B being a function of A. But the logical relation between the two is asymmetric. The present does not cause the past, but the past does cause the present. We then have the following logical postulate: *A cause always precedes its result.* Unfortunately, real models should apply to accounting variables which are observed as a vector in a certain time-period. For statistically observed accounting variables, the concept of simultaneous, interdependent relationships, cannot well be denied.

We now come to what is generally known as Wold's [62] causal chain requirement. Which is in fact also Tinbergen's [57]. Wold considers a logical ordering of the jointly dependent variables within each time-period, *as if* they occurred one after each other. In this connection, Wold uses the term 'uni-relations'. Causal chain models can be solved by a chain of recursive substitutions. Once we know the initial conditions and the exogenous influences, we can calculate (solve) the 'first' variable. We then substitute this solution for the first variable in all other equations, and solve for the 'second' variable, etcetera. The matrix of coefficients for the jointly dependent variables, will be triangular, with unity coefficients on the diagonal. For instance, for a system of order five we might have:

$$A = \begin{bmatrix} 1 & 0 & 0 & 0 & 0 \\ \alpha & 1 & 0 & 0 & 0 \\ \alpha & \alpha & 1 & 0 & 0 \\ \alpha & \alpha & \alpha & 1 & 0 \\ \alpha & \alpha & \alpha & \alpha & 1 \end{bmatrix}$$

Another desirable property of causal chain models is that estimates of these coefficients will not be subject to simultaneous estimation bias.

Unfortunately, as recognised duly by Wold himself, the causal chain requirement may still be impractical, even in its modified form. Consider a simple Keynesian multiplier model

$$p_t = c_t + i_t$$
$$c_t = \alpha \, p_t$$

Real models will of course have a more complicated structure. There will be a public sector and a foreign sector; accordingly, there will be tax and balance of payments leaks. But some degree of multiplier-type feedback by which part of consumers expenditure comes back to the consumers, via production and income, and is spent again *in the same period*, is what we believe to be the working of a real economy.

Accordingly, we cannot exclude it from our models.

Wold [62] himself mentions a second exception "In market models in the form of interdependent systems it is a typical assumption that demand d_t and supply s_t are in instantaneous equilibrium, $d_t = s_t$, so that if this quantity is denoted q_t the model will have two behaviour relationships for q_t. Hence the model cannot be written in the recursive form."

I should like to take exception to this exception. The concept of supply can be meaningful in a national accounting type of model, only if it is related to the supply of production factors, real capital and labour. On the other hand, production (demand), is commonly defined via the accounting system, as sold output. To equate the two[1] defines away the problem of the variation of output, within existing capacity. The alternative approach is of course to postulate demand functions for production factors. The demand for production factors is then a function of, among other things, the state of capacity utilization. Following the general argument of the causal chain approach, it would be desirable if capacity-induced demand for production factors should always be a *lagged* reaction of past changes in output.

Another argument for the same proposition concerns the technical methods of producing. The decision to increase the production capacity of a specific unit of production will incur new fixed cost. Accordingly, it is unlikely to be taken à la minute. Also, in the case of new capital equipment, its implementation may take time.

I would, however, not want to go as far as to formulate a strict requirement in this respect. What matters is that a short-term model should take account of the *possibility* of variation within existing capacity.

Example
The following arrow-scheme might give a simplified picture of the description of a dynamic adjustment process.

At constant prices, we might have:

104

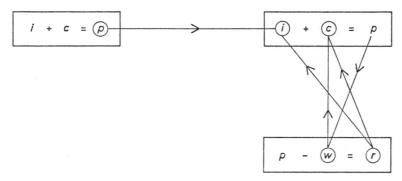

Fig. 2.

The essential reaction-equations of this model are:

Inside each time-period a set of expenditure-multiplier relations, notably: c = consumption being a function of the two categories of functional income (w = wages for income from employment, and r = remainder income for profits). i = investment being partially (but not fully) explained as a function of current profits; with a feedback of production on employment. And, of course, there is the definitial relation between expenditure, production and income.

The essential dynamic relation is the accelerator-type of relation between investment and past production. One might of course also consider a lagged labour demand function, but the example assumes a non-lagged one. Of course a realistic model will be more complicated than the above. The accounting scheme is over-simplified, and we did not indicate any distributed lags, whereas in fact there will be distributed lags. Then, the model assumes constant prices. A price-cost relation could be woven into a model as indicated above, without too much complication. Prices would of course influence the volume of demand. But the real problem is the feedback of volume on price. The other possible entrepreneural reaction on a situation where demand is pressing on the supply capacity would be to increase the price. From that point of view one would want to describe the price mechanism as an adaptive process as well.

But there is a difference. The implementation of a decision to increase the technical capacity to produce, takes time, owing to technical reasons. This is not so with price adjustment. As a result the competing model of

105

the price being purely a function of cost-factors, has a much stronger case than the explanation of current output by a production function. Also, the interdependence between price and volume is complicated by the possibility of anticipation. There might be anticipation of price change, (speculation) as well as anticipation of volume change; the observed price leading instead of lagging.

The fact that we cannot easily establish what precisely is the timing of the price-adjustment mechanism, should not let us lose sight of one important fact: Price-adaptation may have an important stabilizing effect. The multiplier effects of a demand-impulse may be reduced by price-adjustment. Consider the following simplified model:

List of variables

$$pro, PRO = \text{production in volume/value}$$
$$c \quad C = \text{consumption in volume/value}$$
$$g_t = \text{exogenous expenditure}$$
$$i = \text{investment (volume only)}$$
$$L = \text{Wage-bill or labour-value}$$
$$R = \text{remainder income (profits)}$$

The model will now be:

$$pro_t = c_t + i_t + g_t$$
$$PRO_t = L_t + R_t$$
$$PRO_t = pro_t \cdot pri_t \quad \text{\} \quad \text{definition identities}$$
$$C_t = c_t \cdot pri_t$$
$$C_t = 0.9L_t \quad \text{consumption function}$$
$$R_t = 0.6L_t + 1.3\,(pro_t - pro_{t-2})$$

income-distribution relation in lieu of a price equation

$$i_t = 0.3 \times 4\,(pro_{t-1} - pro_{t-2}) + 0.7i_{t-1}$$

flexible accelerator investment demand function with capital output ratio of 4 and adjustment fraction of 0.3

Of the 9 current variables

$$pro_t,\ c_t,\ i_t,\ g_t C_t,\ PRO_t,\ L_t,\ R_t \text{ and } pri_t,$$

L_t and g_t will be exogenous, the rest endogenous. At constant prices, this model will generate explosive oscillations. The reason is that one additional unit of (exogenous) demand, g_t, will cause a more than equal amount of demand for investment goods in a number of succeeding periods, which

106

will be damped down by the autoregressive term of less than unity, only at a much higher level. In the value model, this mechanism is damped yet a bit more by price adjustment. For an additional unit of exogenous demand there will be a partial compensation by way of a reduction in consumption because of rising prices. As a result, there will not be one full unit of additional volume-output in the first place. The dynamic feedback on investment is reduced correspondingly; the additional units of investment do not correspond to a full additional unit of output and the cumulative process of acceleration does not occur to the same degree as it would be in the constant price model.

The price-mechanism may work as a built-in stabilizer. The stabilization is not fully effective since the model is still unstable, but to a lesser degree than the constant prices version.

7.3. THE CUMULATIVE FORECAST[2]

Models should be judged by their outcome, and that outcome is *not* just the single one-period forecast.

The model describes a process[3] of dynamic adjustment. This process, as described by the model, can be judged by generating a consecutive series of hypothetical forecasts.

In this connection, the one-period model is best formulated as

$$A_0 \, \mathbf{y}_t = A_1 \, \mathbf{y}_{t-1} + B \, \mathbf{x}_t \qquad (7.3.1)$$

Here y_t is a vector of currently dependent variables; $\mathbf{x}_t$ is a vector of currently exogenous variables. This specification does in fact include the possibility of longer time-lags.

From (7.3.1) we have the reduced form

$$\mathbf{y}_t = A_0^{-1} A_1 \, \mathbf{y}_{t-1} + A_0^{-1} B \, \mathbf{x}_t \qquad (7.3.2)$$

In order to simplify our notation, we will *denote*

$$A_0^{-1} A_1 = A \qquad (7.3.3)$$

and

$$A_0^{-1} B = C \qquad (7.3.4)$$

The reduced form (7.3.2) may then be written as

$$\mathbf{y}_t = C\mathbf{x}_t + A\mathbf{y}_{t-1} \qquad (7.3.5)$$

Lagged influences of dependent variables of period $t-2$ and exogenous variables of period $t-1$ can be introduced in the current period, as artificial variables. For example, the real specification might give a lagged influence of the production of two periods back. We would then write a definition-identity

$$lp_t = p_{t-1} \qquad \qquad (7.3.ex.1)$$

Here l_p stands for 'lagged production' and p for production. Then wherever we find an influence of p_{t-2}, we write lp_{t-1} instead. This brings longer lags within the reach of a one-period matrix model. The device may be repeated recursively. If a three-period lag is in fact specified we will define a second artificial variable

$$llp_t = lp_{t-1} \qquad \qquad (7.3.ex.2)$$

and write llp_{t-1} everywhere where the real specification gives a non-zero coefficient for p_{t-3}.

By back-substitution for $\mathbf{y}_{t-1}$ by (7.3.5) into (7.3.5) itself we get

$$\mathbf{y}_t = C\mathbf{x}_t + AC\mathbf{x}_{t-1} + A^2\,\mathbf{y}_{t-2} \qquad \qquad (7.3.6)$$

By a process of recursive back-substitution we will then have

$$\mathbf{y}_t^{\,} = \sum_{r=0}^{k} A^r\,C\,\mathbf{x}_{t-r} + A^{k+1}\mathbf{y}_{t-k-1} \qquad \qquad (7.3.7)$$

where k can have any non-negative integer value ($k=0, 1, 2, 3\dots$).

The purpose of (7.3.7) is not so much to obtain any actual forecasts[4] except for low[5] values of k.

If k is at all large, the cumulative forecast is subject to a cumulatively increasing degree of uncertainty. The forecast which we will believe will be the outcome of a purpose-constructed long-term model, or of a simple extrapolation. But the (short-term) model should not 'run mad' and produce unbelievable forecasts. If the model forecasts negative consumption and half of the production going into inventories, we will know there is something wrong with the model, even if that refers to a 100-years cumulative forecast. We will then also suspect some element of irrealism with forecasts on a shorter time-span.

108

7.4. THE LONG-RUN EQUILIBRIUM

The 'inventing' of a longer series of values for a vector of exogenous variables and the subsequent evaluation of the result is a somewhat tedious process.

Under certain assumptions, this process may be replaced by an analytic criterion. The most simple case arises if we may assume that the exogenous variables have a *common* time-trend. In that case they may be replaced by $m+1$ parameters, m levels and one common rate of growth.

One then postulates

$$\mathbf{x}_{t-1} = \gamma^{-1} \mathbf{x}_t \tag{7.4.1}$$

Here γ represents the growth-trend; for example, $\gamma = 1.05$ means 5% per period. We now substitute this expression in the cumulative forecasting formula (7.3.7), to obtain

$$\mathbf{y}_t = \sum_{r=0}^{k} [\gamma^{-1}A]^r \, C \, \mathbf{x}_t + A^{k+1} \, \mathbf{y}_{t-k-1} \tag{7.4.2}$$

We will now *assume* that this series converges, that for large r, $[\gamma^{-1}A]^r$ will vanish. Then for large k, (7.4.2) will converge into

$$\mathbf{y}_t = \sum_{r=0}^{\infty} [\gamma^{-1}A]^r \, C \, \mathbf{x}_t = [I - \gamma^{-1}A]^{-1} \, C \, \mathbf{x}_t \tag{7.4.3}$$

The vector $\mathbf{y}_t$, as obtained by means of (7.4.3), will of course not be identical with the vector $\mathbf{y}_t$, as actually observed.

In (7.4.3), $\mathbf{y}_t$ is computed by the model relative to a somewhat special assumption about the data.

We will now investigate the degree of correspondence between the two.

Example
Consider the following model for a closed economy:

$$p_t = c_t + i_t + g_t$$

$$c_t = \tfrac{1}{2} p_{t-1} + cau_t$$

$$i_t = 0.1 \, (p_{t-1} - c_t) + 0.1 \, i_{t-1} + 0.4 \, (p_{t-1} - p_{t-2})$$

Legenda. p = production; c = consumption; cau = autonomous part of

109

consumption; i=investment; g=exogenous expenditure, mainly government.

The consumption is a lagged function of the previous periods production, via personal income. Investment is a mixture of a savings function (lagged production less consumption), and a flexible acceleration-type relation. We first write out the tableau[6] of the structural coefficients (Table XXVIII):

TABLE XXVIII

p_t	lp_t	i_t	c_t	$=$	p_{t-1}	lp_{t-1}	i_{t-1}	c_{t-1}	$+$	g_t	cau_t
1		-1	-1							1	
	1					1					
		1	.1		.5	$-.4$	.1				
			1		.5						1

The influence of production, lagged two periods, is represented as a one-period lagged influence of the artificial variable 'lagged production'. The reduced form of this model will be

$$
\begin{array}{c}
p_t = \\
lp_t = \\
i_t = \\
c_t =
\end{array}
\begin{bmatrix}
.950 & -.400 & .100 & - & 1.000 & .900 \\
1.000 & - & - & - & - & - \\
.450 & -.400 & .100 & - & - & -.100 \\
.500 & - & - & - & - & 1.000
\end{bmatrix}
$$

with column headings p_{t-1}, lp_{t-1}, i_{t-1}, c_{t-1}, g_t, cau_t.

We now assume a 5% growth rate of the exogenous variables public expenditure and autonomous consumption.

We now compute

$$
[I - 0.95\,A]^{-1} =
\begin{bmatrix}
.098 & .380 & -.095 & - \\
-.950 & 1.000 & - & - \\
-.427 & .380 & .905 & - \\
-.475 & - & - & 1.000
\end{bmatrix}^{-1}
$$

$$
=
\begin{bmatrix}
2.212 & -.929 & 232 & - \\
2.102 & .117 & 221 & - \\
.162 & -.488 & 1.122 & - \\
1.051 & -.441 & .110 & 1.000
\end{bmatrix}
$$

110

After post-multiplication of this inverse with the two right-hand side columns for exogenous expenditure and autonomous consumption, one obtains:

$$
[I - 0.95A]^{-1}
\begin{bmatrix}
1.000 & .900 \\
- & - \\
- & -.100 \\
- & 1.000
\end{bmatrix}
=
\begin{matrix}
 & & g_t & cau_t \\
p_t & & & \\
lp_t & & & \\
i_t & & & \\
c_t & & &
\end{matrix}
\begin{bmatrix}
2.212 & 1.968 \\
2.102 & 1.870 \\
.162 & .034 \\
1.051 & 1.935
\end{bmatrix}
$$

We will now want to analyse the result. The most salient outcome is the low relative level of investment. Even if we assume a zero level of the autonomous consumption, investment is only 7.2% of production. This is a very low figure relative to a growth rate of 5%. It assumes an incremental capital-output ratio of only 1.44.

For a consumption-led expansion it would be even lower, a difference which is somewhat strange in itself.

Ex post, it is not difficult to assess that the investment-equation cannot be a realistic one, at least not on the basis of these parameters. If we put consumption at about $\frac{2}{3}$ of last period's production, the term $0.1(p_{t-1} - c_t)$ will explain a level of investment of about 3% of production. The remainder then will have to come from the accelerator effect.

But the auto-regressive term $0.1i_{t-1}$ is so low [7] that it makes hardly any difference with a fixed accelerator. Hence, the low estimate of the capital-output-ratio, which is substantially the 0.4.

One might argue that this could in fact be known at the outset. And so it could: at least if we assume the specification was written on the basis of a well-established theoretical model. We would then have rejected the statistical estimate of the relation, because it did not satisfy the a priori expectation about the order of magnitude of the coefficients. But suppose one had written the relation, merely on the basis of some sort of idea of a number of different effects, without a precise higher-order model.

Not all 'strange' long-term solutions by (7.4.3) should for that reason alone, lead to a rejection of the corresponding short-term forecasting model. The assumption that all exogenous variables have *one* common trend, may be unrealistic.

For example, the population (manpower) may increase with only $\frac{1}{2}$% a year, while the value of world trade increases with about 8% a year. If we now assume that from now on they move in line at the same trend of 3%, we may well find a 'strange' outcome, which is nevertheless legitimate, and indeed realistic relative to the unrealistic assumptions. In that case (7.4.1) should be replaced by

$$\mathbf{x}_{t-1} = R\mathbf{x}_t \tag{7.4.4}$$

where R is a diagonal matrix of growth parameters (reciprocals of growth-rates).

For example

$$R = \begin{bmatrix} 0.95 & & \\ & 0.99 & \\ & & 0.98 \end{bmatrix}$$

will inform us of the fact that the first exogenous variable grows at 5% per period; the second at 1% and the third at 2%.

In that case, we will have, instead of [8] (7.4.3):

$$\mathbf{y}_t^" = \sum_{r=0}^{\infty} A^r \, CR^r \, \mathbf{x}_t \tag{7.4.5}$$

One can of course evaluate this series numerically, if it is convergent. But I am not aware of any simple analytical formula for its evaluation. The results of (7.4.5) may of course be analysed in a similar way as (7.4.3).

7.5. THE PROBLEM OF STABILITY

In the previous section, we have assumed that the power series

$$I + \gamma^{-1} A + (\gamma^{-1}A)^2 + (\gamma^{-1}A)^3 + \cdots$$

will converge to $[I - \gamma^{-1}A]^{-1}$.

However, unlike the corresponding power series for the input-output inverse, there is no compelling reason why this should be so.

In fact, it is not at all difficult to write a model for which this series will *not* converge. But we would want to disbelieve the outcome of such a model. It is a question of what we believe to be the behaviour of a real economy. One might want to argue that the real economy is not stable there being a business-cycle. Against this proposition, the following coun-ter-arguments should be placed.

Firstly, as shown by Frank and Irma Adelman in their Econometrica article [1] one does not need an unstable model in the mathematical sense, to explain the presence of cyclical fluctuations. A damped oscillatory model, in combination with random shocks in the order of magnitude of the observed random error of the stochastic relations, may generate a pattern of cyclical fluctuation, not unlike the business cycle in the real world. Secondly, there is the balance of payments leak. Already the import leak as such has a stabilising effect. On top of this comes the monetary effect. Unless one assumes an infinitely elastic supply of credit, a deficit on the balance of payments will reduce the amount of money in circulation in a country. It is therefore legitimate for a model for an open economy to be stable, relative to a stable trend in exports. Actual exports will however be subject to non-random fluctuation, originating in the working of a world-wide trade-cycle [36].

We will then normally assume that a model does converge. Mathematically, the concept of the stability of a model is mostly defined relative to a stable *level* of the exogenous variables. We assume convergence of (7.4.3) relative to $\gamma = 1$.

The relation

$$\mathbf{y}_t = [I - \gamma^{-1}A]^{-1} C \mathbf{x}_t \tag{7.5.1}$$

is still an equilibrium condition, relative to a constant rate of growth. This follows by substituting for

$$\mathbf{y}_{t-1} \quad \text{as} \quad \gamma^{-1}\mathbf{y}_t \quad \text{into (7.3.5),} \quad \text{and solving for } \mathbf{y}_t$$

The following may now be observed about the path towards the equilibrium. The relationship

$$A\mathbf{u}_j = \mathbf{u}_j\mu_j \quad (j = 1, 2 \ldots n) \tag{7.5.2}$$

will define n possible *rates of convergence* and corresponding dimensions of disequilibrium. Here n is the order of A.

Example

The model

$$p_t = 6 + 0.8\, p_{t-1} \tag{7.5.ex.1}$$

will have an equilibrium solution $p_t = (1 - 0.8)^{-1}\, 6 = 30$ and a rate of convergence of 0.8 if the initial solution is different from 30.

113

With A being of order one, there will of course be only one dimension of disequilibrium.

In the general case, we allow n dimensions of disequilibrium. If they are independent from one another, we can *always* find n arbitrary parameters w_j $(j=1,2 \ldots n)$, such that an arbitrary initial solution will satisfy

$$\mathbf{y}_t = [I - \gamma^{-1}A]^{-1} C\mathbf{x}_t + \sum_{j=1}^{n} w_j \mathbf{u}_j \mu_j^t \qquad (7.5.3)$$

The μ_j will be solved as the roots of the determinantal equation

$$|A - \mu_j I| = 0 \qquad (7.5.4)$$

so that

$$A \mathbf{u}_j - \mathbf{u}_j \mu_j = 0 \qquad (7.5.5)$$

by (7.5.2) will admit a non-trivial solution.

This amounts to a decomposition of $(\mathbf{y}_t)$ in a number of components, of which one component satisfies the equilibrium condition (7.5.1) and each of the remaining endogenous components satisfy

$$\mathbf{y}_t(j) = \mathbf{u}\, \mu_j^t\, w_j \qquad (7.5.6)$$

where $\mathbf{y}_t(j)$ is the jth component of the path at time t.

Since the exogenous variables are already accounted for in the central equilibrium path, these endogenous vectors must satisfy

$$\mathbf{y}_t(j) = A\, \mathbf{y}_{y-1}(j) \qquad (7.5.7)$$

or, by (7.5.6) and (7.5.7)

$$A\, \mathbf{y}_{t-1}(j) = \mathbf{y}_{t-1}(j)\, \mu_j \qquad (7.5.8)$$

From (7.5.6), (7.5.7) and (7.5.8) we have again (7.5.5).

Example

Consider the stability of the model discussed (as example) in Section 7.4. The latent roots (rates of convergence) are then defined by the requirement

$$\begin{vmatrix} .950 - \lambda & -.400 & .100 & - \\ 1.000 & -\lambda & - & - \\ .450 & -.400 & .100 - \lambda & - \\ .500 & - & - & -\lambda \end{vmatrix} = 0$$

One root of this equation is established at a glance. For $\lambda = 0$ the last column (consumption) will become a zero column.

Otherwise a sufficient condition for singularity will be:

$$\begin{vmatrix} .950 - \lambda & -.400 & .100 \\ 1.000 & -\lambda & - \\ .450 & -.400 & .100 - \lambda \end{vmatrix} = 0$$

The equivalence of the singularity of the total 4×4 matrix with the singularity of the smaller 3×3 matrix is readily verified; one just develops the total determinant by the minors of the last column.

We now develop (minus) the determinant of the smaller 3×3 matrix, by the minors of the middle row, and require:

$$1.000 \begin{vmatrix} -.400 & .100 \\ -.400 & .100 - \lambda \end{vmatrix} + \lambda \begin{vmatrix} .950 - \lambda & .100 \\ .450 & .100 - \lambda \end{vmatrix} = 0$$

or

$$(.400\lambda - .040 + .040) + \lambda \, (\lambda^2 - 1.050\lambda + .095 - .045) = 0$$

or

$$\lambda^3 - 1.050\lambda^2 + .450\lambda = 0$$

We now find a second zero root.

On inspection of the right-hand-side matrix of the structural system, we will see that this could be expected.

The matrix

$$A_1 = \begin{bmatrix} - & - & - & - \\ 1 & - & - & - \\ 0.5 & -0.4 & 0.1 & - \\ 0.5 & - & - & - \end{bmatrix}$$

has the rank two; one column is a zero vector and two of the other columns are proportional. As a result, $A = A_0^{-1} A_1$ will also be of rank two. Two remainder non-zero roots are now to be solved from

$$\lambda^2 - 1.05\lambda + 0.450 = 0$$

This equation solves a pair of complex roots

$$\lambda_{3,4} = 0.525 \pm 0.418 \, i$$

The interpretation of the roots will be as follows. One zero root corresponds to the 'possibility' of the initial situation being just consumption and nothing else. This amounts to a negation of a non-dynamic relation, in this case the accounting identity. *This* element of disequilibrium will be corrected at once, hence reduce to zero. The next zero root corresponds to having initial conditions:

$$p_{t-1} = 0; \quad lp_{t-1} = 1; \quad i_{t-1} = 4; \quad c_{t-1} = -4$$

It is readily verified that this direction of disequilibrium is adjusted by the model, at once. (The dependent variables with index t can be solved by recursive substitution, and will all be zero.)

The remaining pair of complex roots represents a cyclical oscillation with a period length of $2\pi(\text{arctang } .418/.525)^{-1} = 9.35$. The absolute value of the root is $\sqrt{(.525^2 + .418^2)} = 0.67$. This pair of roots will then give rise to a damped oscillation.

The corresponding pair of vectors will of course be complex as well and will define the relative level and phase of the different accounting variables relative to the general cycle.

Inferences concerning the *length* of the cyclical fluctuations are of course an important by-product of the stability-analysis.

7.6. THE 'SIMPLE' LONG-TERM MODEL

In 1966 Waelbroeck [60] wrote: "This kind of model is of a fairly simple mathematical structure, concentrating on an input-output table. It has been initiated by French planners, and since been adopted in a number of countries.

Undoubtedly, it is still the core of a programming-approach towards medium-term planning, for it is excellently suited for a process of dialogue between the government on the one side and the private sector of the economy on the other side." (See also Section 6.4.)

We are now in a position to indicate some of the reasons why 'this kind of model' is as it is.

First of all, the forecasting of the specific path of dynamic adjustment for a period of five years and upwards, becomes a somewhat meaningless exercise. Then one assumes away most of the problems of short-term dynamic adjustment, and concentrates on the terminal solution only. The replacement of adaptive-type relations by cruder equilibrium conditions will result in a certain simplification of the model. In particular, the standard assumption is that output and production capacity are the same variable. The demand for production factors is related to a production function and not to factor-demand functions of the adaptive type.

The problem of how the model is to adapt itself during the period is defined away by *assuming*[9] a specific (linear or exponential) time-path. The actual path during the period is the subject of a short-term model, which must then be of a more refined structure. Because of this simplification, the long-term model can consider a sectorwise breakdown more easily than the short-term model. To forecast levels of production, inventories interindustry deliveries and investment by origin and destination for 20 sectors, for 5 or more successive years, would be a very big job indeed. This would be particularly so if it was taken seriously; if one would want to determine the specific position of each sector in a realistic way, not just as a certain function of the macro-economic accounting variables.

One would have to take into account a different pattern of lags in the adaptive behaviour of each sector.

The simplifying assumption of the long-term model, which defines away any oscillatory behaviour during the period, really does help.

NOTES TO CHAPTER VII

* A paper, which is substantially this chapter, less Section 7.5, with an additional introduction, will also appear under the title "Short versus long-term economy models" [27a].

[1] Yet, I understand this is in fact being done by some practitioners. See Klein *et al.* [33].

[2] See also Goldberger [20], p. 373.

[3] Accordingly, there is a case for a method of simultaneous estimation, which relates the estimates of model-parameters to the fit of the sample-periods cumulative 'forecasts'.

[4] Yet this was done by Van den Beld [3].

[5] The special case of 'forecasting' initial conditions, for which the statistics are not yet available, will arise. See Heesterman [27].

[6] Note, that the model satisfies the causal chain requirement.

[7] A flexible accelerator, without a financial component, would be

$$i_t = \alpha\kappa(p_{t-1} - p_{t-2}) + (1 - \alpha)\,i_{t-1}$$

where κ is the capital-output ratio, and α an adjustment-percentage; entrepreneurs are assumed to adjust capacity to sold output to a fraction of α, which would in this case be 90%.

[8] In fact it is almost standard procedure to formulate short-term forecasting models in terms of percentage increments of the accounting variables.

The main reason for this practice is that it allows estimates of the structural relations to be free of heteroscedasticity, as well as of positive serial correlation of the error term. Definition identities must of course be approximated by means of the Taylor expansion. Now if this method is followed, one can simply apply (7.4.3), with $\gamma = 1$. Different growth-rates of exogenous variables are now fed in as 'levels' of the (changes in) accounting variables. The outcome for the dependent variables will then of course also be in terms of percentage increments; which can be compared with their average increments (trend) over the sample period.

[9] In fact a fixed accelerator-type of investment demand is implied by the combination of capacity being equal to sold output and the use of a capital output ratio. This is *not* normally a converging adjustment mechanism. (See Section 6.3.)

CHAPTER VIII

FORECAST AND POLICY

8.1. DATA AND INSTRUMENTS

We assume now that we have a model. We want to make a decision to formulate economic policy. Relative to the model, we will know what the value of the dependent variables will be, once we know what the value of the exogenous variables will be.

The exogenous variables fall into two classes. There are the *instruments* which can be fixed at will by the policy-maker. They are directly under his control. Obvious examples of instruments are the rates of the various types of taxes. The other group are the *data*. A special group of data are the lagged influences of past values of accounting variables. The knowledge of these data is a question of having up-to-date statistics. But not all data-variables are of this kind. There are also events in the current time-period which have an influence on the dependent variables without themselves being explained by the model. Examples are the weather, the state of foreign markets etc. For these variables a forecast, a 'higher order forecast' is required. This higher-order forecast is then made by other methods than with the help of the model.

Methods of making a higher-order forecast include: simple extrapolation, guess, and analysis of statements of other policy-makers.

A variable may of course be a datum relative to (outside the control of) the user of the model, but *in* the control of some other decision maker. Even when this other decision maker is not prepared to adjust his decision, he may be prepared to reveal his intention. Examples are foreign budgets, and surveys of investment plans by major firms.

The policy decision will now consist in establishing suitable values of the instrument variables. Together with the data-variables, which must be assumed to be known or approximately known, this makes the level of all the accounting variables determinate, by the model.

8.2. THE POLICY PROGRAMMING PROBLEM

In the context of the making of a policy decision, the model is best formulated as

$$Ay = Bx + Cz \qquad (8.2.1)$$

Here y are the dependent variables, x the instruments and z the data. Logically, the question of the optimal choice of policy is a programming problem.

Maximize[1]

$$\tau (y, x),$$

subject to

$$Ay - Bx = Cz \qquad (8.2.2)$$

where τ is the preference-function, the objective function. Logical as this approach may be, it is not a particularly fruitful approach towards obtaining an actual policy decision.

First, we have to specify the preference function. This assumes that the policy maker *has* such a thing as a general preference function. It also assumes that he and his adviser, the econometrician, are capable between the two, to write the function on paper as a certain mathematical function, complete with figures for the coefficients.

The most simple case would be a *linear* function. Unfortunately, this is not a particularly realistic preference function. A linear programme finds its solution in a cornerpoint; hence for each non-zero level of an instrument, a dependent variable is driven out of the basis, and its zero value is listed as the most preferred level.

It is most unlikely that this is really the preferred solution. Most policy makers would prefer to avoid any radical changes, relative to a satisfactory set of initial conditions. Any realistic preference function is essentially non-linear. Also, most likely, the model would no longer be applicable for any really strong change in policy. The model as such may give a conditional forecast relative to the complete abolishment of all indirect taxes, at the same time increasing the direct taxes with a factor two.

But if the model forecast would really come true after the adoption of such legislation, that is another matter. More likely, the result would be a change of government, as well as a number of unexpected economic results.

120

8.3. TINBERGEN'S METHOD OF INSTRUMENTS AND TARGETS

Firstly, we introduce the concept of an 'absolute target'. Instead of specifying a preference function, one simply formulates a requirement. Certain 'important' policy variables such as employment, consumption, the balance of payments, are to be at such and such a level and no other. The levels of these variables are then the *targets*.

The collection of instruments is now split into two groups. This introduces the notion of a political boundary condition. Instruments are restricted to a limited range of variation only. This will prevent the kind of 'runaway solution' just discussed above. But this is not yet a wholly satisfactory solution. Suppose the boundary condition is set at a level which is really a boundary, which cannot be surpassed under any circumstances.

Income-tax cannot be increased by more than 20% in any year because this will cause a fall of the government. Even so, it may be felt undesirable to increase income tax by more than 5%, while a 1% increase is not a matter of particular political importance, relative to the alternative of a small rise in the price-level.

Some instruments are now specified at a particular numerical level. The remaining group of instruments should be of the same number as the targets, so that they can be solved by inversion of a linear system. One partitions and re-orders (8.2.1) as follows:

$$A_1\mathbf{y}_1 - B_1\mathbf{x}_1 = -A_2\mathbf{y}_2 + B_2\mathbf{x}_2 + C\mathbf{z} \qquad (8.3.1)$$

Here $\mathbf{y}_2$ are the target variables, and instruments $\mathbf{x}_2$ have been set a priori at more or less definite values. $\mathbf{x}_1$ should be of the same order as $\mathbf{y}_2$ so that the composite matrix $[A_1 B_1]$ remains square. Obviously, the partitioning should be such that $[A_1 B_1]$ is not only square, but also non-singular.

The method is normally applied relative to a (preliminary) conditional forecast, which is in some respect unsatisfactory. This preliminary forecast is the 'no policy' forecast. One begins to assume that all instruments are at a level they would have without any conscious political action. Tax rates are unchanged, the wage rate is at the level it would attain without public interference, etcetera. We will then identify the *undesirable* outcomes of such a policy.

Example

First, consider a somewhat simplified version of the short-term forecasting model, as discussed in Chapter II. We will assume all prices except for the exogenous wage-rate. Also, we have in fact somewhat altered the coefficients. The resulting instruments columns of the reduced form are now as follows:

TABLE XXIX

	w'	giv'	gl'	$LTAU'$	$PTAU'$
L'	9.39	0.19	1.14	-0.19	-0.13
p'	2.88	0.89	1.64	-0.87	-0.59
c'	6.89	0.24	0.72	-1.09	-0.56
iv'	0.31	0.09	0.16	-0.09	-0.26
st'	–	–	–	–	–
e'	-4.50	–	–	–	–
im'	-0.18	0.44	0.24	-0.30	-0.23
l'	0.79	0.19	1.14	-0.19	-0.13
SL'	7.42	0.08	0.45	-1.07	-0.05
SP'	1.44	0.45	0.82	-0.44	-1.29

Legenda

dependent variables: L=labour in value (wage bill), p' is production in volume; c=consumption; iv= (private) investment in fixed assets; st= stock accumulation; e=export; im=import (all in volume); l=labour in volume; SL=spendable income from labour; SP=spendable income from profits.

instruments: w=wage rate; giv=governments investment; gl=governments employment; $LTAU'$=autonomous change in taxes on earned income, by means of change in rates; $PTAU'$=idem for profits.

The prime will indicate that all *variables are in terms of changes*. We now suppose that the 'no policy' forecast shows the 'undesirable' feature of a billion balance of payments deficit. One will now want to restore balance of payments equilibrium. This then gives rise to the formulation of a target:

$$e' - im' = 1$$

We further suppose the 'no policy' forecast of employment to be at a fairly satisfactory level of full employment; we do not want to jeopardize this by deflationary policies. And neither do we want any further increase in the demand for labour by export stimulating measures, since this would lead to inflationary pressures. Our second target is then

$$l' = 0.$$

We have no special interest in the other dependent variables L', p', c', iv', st', SL' and SP', at least not within the range of variation that is likely to be relevant, as a result of our balance of payments problem.

These variables are then the *irrelevant variables*. The *data* will of course remain unchanged relative to the 'no policy' forecast.

We now have from the instruments block-column of the reduced form:

$$e' - im' = -4.32\, w' - 0.44\, giv' - 0.24\, gl' + 0.30\, LTAU' +$$
$$0.23\, PTAU' = 1$$

and for the employment

$$l' = 0.79\, w' + 0.19\, giv' + 1.14\, gl' - 0.19\, LTAU' + 0.13\, PTAU' = 0$$

We now have a system of 2 equations, with five instruments whose values are as yet to be established.

Three instrument levels can then be fixed without reference to the two equations, after which one can normally solve the remaining two. In this connection, the concept of a political boundary condition will arise. Suppose the government had pledged itself *not* to increase the tax rate on earned income; $LTAU'$ would be restricted to non-positive values only.

Tinbergen seems to assume[2] that policy-makers formulate at least as many targets, as there are "free" instruments, not at a boundary level, and this may be asking the impossible, as one cannot normally have more targets than instruments. The concept of a political boundary condition is of course somewhat fluid. If it should really be seen as urgent, the taxes could be raised despite an earlier pledge not to do so. In fact, it is a question of political preference. The boundary conditions represent a level at which the valuation of an additional unit of this particular variable is assumed to change more or less markedly. The same applies to an absolute target as well. If equilibrium becomes very difficult to attain, one will mitigate the balance of payment requirement, or may aim for the smallest possible deficit. Something very similar to Tinbergen's method may also be used, simply to obtain a consistent forecast, which satisfies certain desiderata, and can be expected to come true as far as the model is valid.

Suppose there are still more 'free' instrument levels than absolute targets. The method then amounts to this: Fix some of the instrument levels arbitrarily. One will normally choose some of the less effective instruments at a 'reasonable' level, making some contribution to the attainment of the target. The remaining collection of instruments should not only be relatively effective in influencing the targets, but also relatively unlike each other. An example of an undesirable combination of remaining 'free' instruments would be the two types of taxes. They would give rise to a subsystem as follows. Denoting the effect of the arbitrarily fixed instruments on the targets, as $(e' - im')^*$ and $l^{*'}$ we would have

$$e' - im' = 0.30 \, LTAU' + 0.23 \, PTAU' + (e' - im')^*$$

$$l' = - 0.19 \, LTAU' - 0.13 \, PTAU' + l^{*'}.$$

This subsystem is not completely singular, but its non-singularity hinges on the relative labour and import intensities of consumption and investment. The major result of both is to influence the general level of economic activity. In the present example, if one assumes that all instruments are free of their boundary conditions, the most efficient combination of two instruments will of course be the wage rate w' and the public employment gl'. Unfortunately, it is common that precisely the more efficient instruments are limited by political boundary conditions. This is particularly so with the problem just discussed above, balance of payments versus full employment. If there is a serious gap between the two, the usual collection of monetary and fiscal instruments will all have somewhat similar effects on both targets. If there is a serious gap between the two, one wants an instrument which will redress the balance of payments without having the usual deflationary effect on employment. But if such an instrument is at all available (incomes policy, exchange control, devaluation[3]) it is often difficult to use it, for political reasons.

8.4. THEIL'S QUADRATIC PROGRAMMING APPROACH

Theil specifies the preference function to be a quadratic form

$$\tau = (\mathbf{y'}, \mathbf{x'}) \, P \begin{pmatrix} \mathbf{y} \\ \mathbf{x} \end{pmatrix} + \mathbf{w'y} + \mathbf{v'z} \tag{8.4.1}$$

Here P is a matrix of coefficients. Theoretically one could conceive P to be a more or less 'ordinary' matrix. But its off-diagonal elements represent the change in our valuation of one variable, as a result of the value of another variable. Normally one would only be in a position to specify meaningful coefficients for a diagonal P.

$\mathbf{w'}$ and $\mathbf{v'}$ represent linear valuations of the dependent variables and instruments. If the corresponding programming problem
maximize τ
subject to

$$Ay - Bx = Cz \tag{8.2.2}$$

is to be convex, and is to have a unique, finite all-positive solution, it is necessary that P is negative semi-definite[4]. In the simplified case of a diagonal matrix P, all the diagonal elements of P will then be negative. The valuation for a particular variable will then be (for a dependent variable)

$$\tau_i = -\alpha_i y_i^2 + \beta_i y_i \tag{8.4.2}$$

This corresponds to a 'preferred value' of $\frac{1}{2}\beta_i/\alpha_i$ for that particular variable.

Theil's approach is of some importance, not because it is a practical way to establish optimal values of instruments, but because of a theorem which results from it. Theil considers the value of the preference function as a random variable, being a function of the exogenous variables and of the random error terms in the structural relations.

Our average expectation of that random error is zero, there is just as much chance of the error being positive or negative. The value of the preference function, which corresponds to this assumption is then named, the value of the expected preference function.

Our approach so far has been to maximize this value of the expected preference function; or to assume that the policy decision which is taken maximizes such a function. We have disregarded the stochastic nature of the model. In fact, non-zero random error will occur. The actual value of the preference function will then be different. Generally, the result will be less preferred than the one that was planned for[5]. The reason is that the policy vector as chosen is imperfectly adapted to the outcome of economic events, which were anticipated by means of an imperfect forecast. This introduces the notion of the (average) expected value of the preference function.

This is the preference value we can expect on the average, as a result of the presence of the random error. The probability distribution of this random error vector is assumed to be known, the usual statistical assumptions are made.

Theil now formulates a somewhat different problem: How can we maximize the expected value of the preference function, duly taking into account the stochastic nature of the model, by the choice of our instruments vector?

Theil has shown that the *same* vector of instruments, maximizes the value of the expected preference function (the non-stochastic case), and as well the expected value of the preference function (the stochastic case). In other words, if the preference function is quadratic, one is justified in disregarding (Theil [53], p. 56) the random component. The 'if' however, is of some importance. Two essential criteria of the quadratic function are: its convexity, and its symmetry. The convexity is a necessary mathematical requirement, and anyhow, well in line with what we know of the behaviour of policy-makers. But this is not the case with the second property, its symmetry.

I suspect most real preference functions – if we assume they exist – to be asymmetric round a preferred value. This is particularly so in the case of balance of payments problems. A surplus in excess of what is seen as necessary is seen with cool complacency, a deficit is a cause for alarm.

Something similar applies to unemployment. In this case, there is an underlying assumption that with over-full employment a different model becomes operative, an inflationary model, while at less than full employment we have a volume model. It is assumed that the inflationary model is non-linear and it is not formulated in an exact way. Instead one wants to stay clear of it, if necessary at considerable cost.

Our beliefs about the behaviour of the economy are then transformed into a non-linear preference function.

NOTES TO CHAPTER VIII

[1] I am aware of *one* successful attempt to formulate a formal preference function and to obtain an at least meaningful outcome. In this case the preference function was presented as a piecewise broken linear function, the points of discontinuity being based on figures, which arose in actual policy discussion. See Van Eijk and Sandee [18].

[2] See Chapter V of *On the Theory of Economic Policy* [56].

[3] The combination of devaluation *and* a dose of deflation at the same time is now seen to be a standard example of the relation between two instruments (the exchange rate and the monetary fiscal package), and two targets, balance of payments equilibrium and full employment without excess demand pressure on production capacity.

The devaluation increases exports, but the corresponding rise in production must be nullified by the internal deflation, so as to reduce domestic expenditure.

[4] The Hessian of the Lagrangean, which corresponds to the Kuhn-Tucker optimality conditions, is $P + P'$. The linear terms, both from the objective function and from the side conditions, will vanish. The negative-definiteness of P or of $P + P'$ are equivalent.

[5] The possibility of an occasional 'windfall', a favourable outcome of events, cannot be excluded.

LIST OF SOME OF THE TABLES AND THE EXAMPLES
TO WHICH THEY BELONG

128

BIBLIOGRAPHY

[1] Adelman, Irma and Adelman, Frank, 'The Dynamic Properties of The Klein-Goldberger Model', *Econometrica*, Oct. 1959. Reprinted in: A.E.A. 'Readings in Business Cycles', Allen and Unwin, London, 1965.

[2] Amundson, A.: 'Private Consumption in Norway, 1930–1970', in *Europe's Future Consumption* (ed. by J. Sandee), (ASEPELT II), North-Holland Publishing Co., Amsterdam, 1964.

[3] Beld, C. A. van den, 'An Experimental Medium Term Model for the Dutch Economy', in C.E.I.R. Ltd., *Mathematical Model Building in Economics and Industry* (collected papers of a conference organized by C.E.I.R. and held in London, 4–6 July 1967). Charles Griffin and Co., London, 1968.

[3a] Bjerkholt, O., 'A Precise Description of the Economic Model Modis III' *Economics of Planning* 8 (1968) 26–56.

[4] Bodewig, E., *Matrix Calculus*, North-Holland Publishing Co., Amsterdam, 1955.

[5] Centraal Plan Bureau, *Centraal Economisch Plan 1955*, Staatsdrukkerij en Uitgeverijbedrijf, The Hague, Netherlands, 1955.

[6] Central Bureau of Statistics, 'Cumulated Cost Ratios for the Netherlands Economy in 1950', *Statistical Studies*, No. 6 (Nov. 1955) No. 6, 3–30.

[7] Central Planning Bureau, *Forecast and Realization; The forecasts by the Netherlands Central Planning Bureau, 1953–1963*, Staatsdrukkerij en Uitgeverijbedrijf, The Hague, 1965.

[8] Central Planning Bureau, *Central Economic Plan 1961* (Annex I; the model), publication as above.

[9] Central Statistical Office, *National Income and Expenditure, 1967*, Her Majesty's Stationary Office, London, 1967.

[10] Chakravarty, S., *The Logic of Investment Planning*, North-Holland Publishing Co., Amsterdam, 1959.

[11] Chenery, H. B., 'Overcapacity and Accelerator Principle', *Econometrica* 20 (1952) 1–28.

[12] Chenery, H. B. and Clark, P. G., *Interindustry Economics*, John Wiley and Sons, New York 1959.

[13] Christ, C. F., *Econometric Models and Methods*, John Wiley and Sons, 1966.

[14] Cohn, P. M., *Linear Equations*, Routledge and Kegan Paul, London, 1958.

[15] Debreu, G. and Herstein, I. N., 'Non-Negative Square Matrices', *Econometrica* 21, 597–607.

[16] Domar, E., 'Expansion and Employment', *American Economic Review*, 37 (1947) 34–55.

[17] Dorfman, R., Samuelson, P., and Solow, R., *Linear Programming and Economic Analysis*, McGraw Hill, 1958.

[18] Eijk, C. J. van and Sandee, J., 'Quantitative Determination of Optimum Economic Policy', *Econometrica* 27 (January 1959) 1–13.

129

[19] Fuller, L. E., *Basic Matrix Theory*, Prentice-Hall, Englewood Cliffs, N.J., 1962.

[20] Goldberger, A. S., *Econometric Theory*, John Wiley and Sons, New York, 1964.

[21] Goldberger A. S., *Impact Multipliers and Dynamic Properties of the Klein-Goldberger Model*, North-Holland Publishing Co., Amsterdam, 1959.

[22] Goodwin, R. M., 'The Nonlinear Accelerator and the Persistence of Business Cycles', *Econometrica* **19** (1951) 1–17.

[23] Harrod, R. F., 'An Essay in Dynamic Theory', *Economic Journal* **49** (April 1939) 14–33.

[24] Harrod, R. F., *Towards a Dynamic Economics*, Macmillan and Co., London, 1948.

[25] Hawkins, D. and Simon, H. A., 'Some Conditions of Macro-Economic Stability', *Econometrica* **17**, 245–248.

[26] Heesterman, A. R. G., 'Input-Output: An Iterative Approach to Planning', *Economics of Planning* **7**, 280–286.

[27] Heesterman, A. R. G., 'Forecasting the Past', *Statistica Neerlandica* **22** (1968) 267–271.

[27a] Heesterman, A. R. G., 'Short versus Long-Term Economy Models', in *Econometric Models of the U.K.* (ed. by K. Hilton). Collected papers of a conference, organized on behalf of the Social Science Research Council, Southampton, 14–17 April 1969. Macmillan and Co., London (Forthcoming).

[28] Hicks, J. R., 'Mr. Harrod's Dynamic Theory', in *American Economic Association Readings in Business Cycle Theory*, Allen and Unwin, London, 1965. (Reprinted from *Econometrica*, May 1949.)

[29] Hicks, J. R., *A Contribution to the Theory of the Trade Cycle*, Clarendon Press, Oxford, 1950.

[30] Johanson, L., 'Substitution Versus Fixed Production Coefficients in the Theory of Economic Growth. A Synthesis', *Econometrica* **27** (1959) 157–176.

[31] Keynes, J. M., *The General Theory of Employment, Interest and Money*, Macmillan and Co., London, 1936.

[32] Klein, L. R. and Goldberger, A. S., *An Econometric Model of the United States 1929–1952*, North-Holland Publishing Co., Amsterdam, 1964.

[33] Klein, L. R., Ball, R. J., Hazelwood, A., and Vandome, P., *An Econometric Model of the United Kingdom*, Basil Blackwell, Oxford, 1961.

[34] Kuznets, S., 'Long Term Trends in Capital Formation Proportion', *Economic Development and Cultural Change*, **9**, (July 1961), No. 4, Part. II, 3–123.

[35] Leontief, W., *The Structure of the American Economy, 1919–1929*, Harvard University Press, 1941.

[36] Leontief, W., *The Structure of the American Economy, 1919–1939*, Oxford University Press, New York, 1951.

[37] Leontief, W. and Hoffenberg, M., 'The Economic Effect of Disarmament', *Sci. Am.*, (April 1961); reprinted as Chapter 9 in: Leontief, W. *Input Output Economics*, Oxford University Press, New York, 1966.

[38] Lecomber, J. R. C., 'A Model of the British Economy', paper presented to the British Computer Society at the University of Warwick, 9 April 1968.

[39] Mattessisch, R., *Accounting and Analytic Methods*, Richard D. Irwin Inc., Homewood, Illinois, 1964.

[40] Meyer, J. R. and Glauber, R. R., 'Investment Decisions, Economic Forecasting and Public Policy', Division of Research, Graduate School of Business Administration, Harvard University, Boston, Mass., 1964.

[41] Polak, J. J. and Rhomberg, R. R., 'Economic Instability in An International Set-

ting', in *American Economic Review* (Papers and Proceedings), vol. LII, May 1962. Reprinted in A.E.A. *Readings in Business Cycles*, Allen and Unwin, London, 1965.

Post, J. J. *and* Verdoorn, P. J. see Verdoorn

[42] Questney, F., 'Tableau Economique', in *Grande Encyclopédie, 1758*, as quoted by: Gide, Gh. and Rist, F. *A History of Economic Doctrines*, Harrap, 1949.

[43] Ricardo, D., *On the Principles of Political Economy and Taxation*, John Murray, London, 1819.

[44] Robinson, Joan, *The Accumulation of Capital*, McMillan and Co., London, 1956.

[45] Sandee, J., 'Possible Economic Growth in The Netherlands', in *Europe's Future in Figures* (ed. by R. C. Geary), (ASEPELT I), North-Holland Publishing Co., Amsterdam, 1962.

[46] Sandee, J., 'A Demonstration Planning Model for India', *Indian Statistical Series*, No. 7.

[47] Smith, Harlan M., Uses of Leontief's open Input-Output Model' in *Activity Analysis of Production and Allocation* (ed. by T. C. Koopmans), Cowles Commission Monograph, No. 13, John Wiley and Sons, 1951.

[48] Solow, R. M., 'Investment and Technical Progress', in Arrow, K. J. and others (editors) *Mathematical Methods in the Social Sciences, Proceedings of a conference etc. (Stanford 1959)* (ed. by K. J. Arrow *et al.*), Stanford University Press, Stanford, 1960.

[49] Solow, R. M., 'Capital Theory and the Rate of Return' (Professor F. de Vries Lecture, Rotterdam), North-Holland Publishing Co., Amsterdam 1960.

[50] Stone, R., 'Linear Expenditure Systems and Demand Analysis: An Application to the Pattern of British Demand, *Economic Journal* 64 (Sept. 1954), 511–527.

[51] Stone, R., *Input-Output and National Accounts*, O.E.C.D. Paris, 1961.

[52] Stone, Richard and Stone, Giovanna, *National Income and Expenditure*, Bowes and Bowes, London, 1966.

[53] Theil, H., *Optimal Decision Rules for Government and Industry*, North-Holland Publishing Co., Amsterdam, 1964.

[54] Theil, H. and Boot, J. C. G., 'The Final Form of Econometric Equation Systems', *Review of the International Statistical Institute*, 30 (1962) 136–152.

[55] Tilanus, C. B. and Rey, G., Input-Output Volume and Value Predictions for the Netherlands', *International Economic Review* 5, 34–45.

[56] Tinbergen, J., *On the Theory of Economic Policy*, North-Holland Publishing Co., Amsterdam, 1955.

[57] Tinbergen, J., *Econometric Business Cycle Research*, Hermann et Cie, Paris, 1937. Reprinted in A.E.A. *Readings in Business Cycle Theory*, Allen and Unwin, London, 1950.

[58] Tinbergen, J., 'An Economic Policy for 1936', paper originally read in Dutch, published in translation in *Jan Tinbergen, Selected papers* (ed. by L. H. Klaassen, L. M. Koyck, and H. J. Witteveen), North Holland Publishing Co., Amsterdam, 1959.

[59] Verdoorn, P. J. and Post, J. J., 'Capacity and Short-Term Multipliers' in Colston Research Society *Econometric Analysis for National Economic Planning* (Colston Papers), Butterworth, London, 1964.

[60] Waelbroeck, J., 'Les applications de l'économétrie à la gestion des affaires publiques', *Revue Belge de Statistique et de Recherche Opérationnelle* 6 (Nos. 3–4) pp. 50–54.

[61] Werf, D. van der, 'A Linear Model to Forecast Short-Term Movements in the West German Economy'. Paper read at the European Meeting, Amsterdam, 2–7 Sept. 1968.

[62] Wold, H. O., 'Forecasting by the Chain Principle' in *Econometric Model Building: Essays in the Casual Chain Approach* (ed. by H. O. Wold), North-Holland Publishing Co., Amsterdam, 1964.